Ohio

interactive SCIENCE

Go to **MyScienceOnline.com** to experience science in a whole new way.

Interactive tools such as My Planet Diary connect you to the latest science happenings.

my planet Diary

- Search **Earth's Journal** for important science news from around the world.
- Use **Earth's Calendar** to find out when cool scientific events occur.
- Explore science **Links** to find even more exciting information about our planet.

Visit **Jack's Blog** to be the first to know about what is going on in science!

PEARSON

Glenview, Illinois • Boston, Massachusetts • Chandler, Arizona • Upper Saddle River, New Jersey

Program Authors

DON BUCKLEY, M.Sc.
Information and Communications Technology Director, The School at Columbia University, New York, New York
A founder of New York City Independent School Technologists (NYCIST) and long-time chair of New York Association of Independent Schools' annual IT conference, Mr. Buckley has taught students on two continents and created multimedia and Internet-based instructional systems for schools worldwide.

ZIPPORAH MILLER, M.A.Ed.
Associate Executive Director for Professional Programs and Conferences, National Science Teachers Association, Arlington, Virginia
Ms. Zipporah Miller is a former K–12 science supervisor and STEM coordinator for the Prince George's County Public School District in Maryland. She is a science education consultant who has overseen curriculum development and staff training for more than 150 district science coordinators.

MICHAEL J. PADILLA, Ph.D.
Associate Dean and Director, Eugene P. Moore School of Education, Clemson University, Clemson, South Carolina
A former middle school teacher and a leader in middle school science education, Dr. Michael Padilla has served as president of the National Science Teachers Association and as a writer of the National Science Education Standards. He is professor of science education at Clemson University.

KATHRYN THORNTON, Ph.D.
Professor and Associate Dean, School of Engineering and Applied Science, University of Virginia, Charlottesville, Virginia
Selected by NASA in May 1984, Dr. Kathryn Thornton is a veteran of four space flights. She has logged more than 975 hours in space, including more than 21 hours of extravehicular activity. As an author on the *Scott Foresman Science* series, Dr. Thornton's enthusiasm for science has inspired teachers around the globe.

MICHAEL E. WYSESSION, Ph.D.
Associate Professor of Earth and Planetary Science, Washington University, St. Louis, Missouri
An author on more than 50 scientific publications, Dr. Wysession was awarded the prestigious Packard Foundation Fellowship and Presidential Faculty Fellowship for his research in geophysics. Dr. Wysession is an expert on Earth's inner structure and has mapped various regions of Earth using seismic tomography. He is known internationally for his work in geoscience education and outreach.

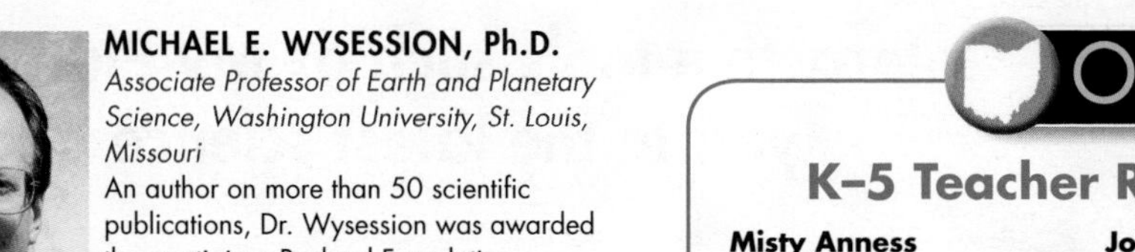

K–5 Teacher Reviewers

Misty Anness
Wilson Elementary School
Cincinnati, Ohio

Sunshine Craven
Liberty Local School District
Liberty, Ohio

Dr. Richard Fairman
Antioch University Midwest
Yellow Springs, Ohio

John Farmer
Ayer Elementary School
Cincinnati, Ohio

Brice Harris
Trumbull County Educational Service Center
Niles, Ohio

Lorraine Turner
Cleveland Heights – University Heights City Schools
University Heights, Ohio

Cover Art: *William Gottlieb/Corbis*

Taken from:

Interactive Science, Grade K
by Don Buckley, M.Sc., Zipporah Miller, M.A.Ed., Michael J. Padilla, Ph.D, Kathryn Thornton, Ph.D., and Michael E. Wysession, Ph.D.

Published by Pearson Education, Inc.
Upper Saddle River, New Jersey 07458

Pearson Learning Solutions, 501 Boylston Street, Suite 900, Boston, MA 02116
A Pearson Education Company
www.pearsoned.com

Printed in the United States of America

8 16

000200010270754507

MH

2017 Realize Edition

ISBN 10: 1-256-14560-2
ISBN 13: 978-1-256-14560-8

Unit A

Science, Engineering, and Technology

The Nature of Science

What is science?

Ohio

Chapter 2

Solve Problems

How can you solve problems?

Unit B
Life Science

Living and Nonliving Things

What can you tell about living things?

Unit C
Earth Science

Earth and Sky

What are Earth and the sky like?

Chapter 5

Unit D
Physical Science

Objects

What are objects like?

About Science

Draw pictures. Write words.

Ohio

Unit
A

Science, Engineering, and Technology

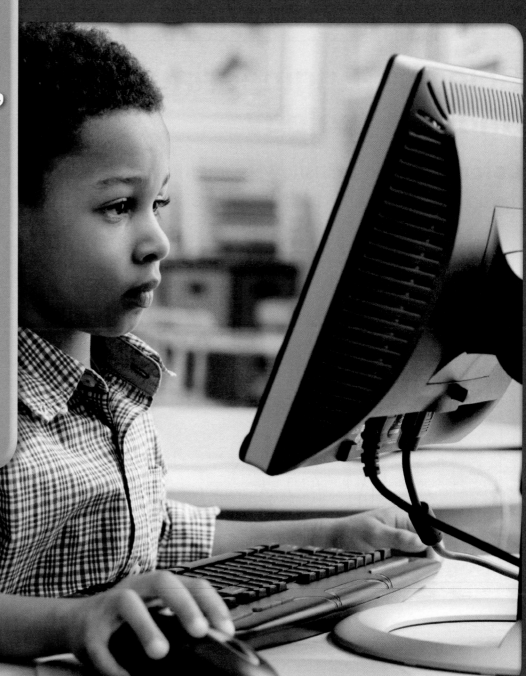

Chapter 1
The Nature of Science

What is science?

Chapter 2
Solve Problems

How can you solve problems?

Computers can help you learn.

Ohio

Name ____________________

Science, Engineering, and Technology

Color a picture that shows something people made to help them go from place to place.

Directions: Discuss the pictures with children. Then ask children to color the picture showing something people made so they can ride from place to place.

Home Activity: Your child is going to study science and technology. Your home is filled with appliances, devices, and machines that are the result of scientific and technological advances. Point out an appliance, device, or machine in your home. Ask your child to name the item and tell what it is used for. Continue with other items.

Ohio
Chapter
1
The Nature of Science
Why is she
looking
so closely?
myscienceonLine.com
THE BIG ?
What is science?

Name ______________________________

What is science?

Draw a picture in the hand lens.

Activity 2
Use with page 2.

Directions: Discuss observation as a practice of science, and talk about what the girl might see through the hand lens. Then have children draw a picture of a flower in the hand lens on this page.

Home Activity: Your child looked at Chapter 1, which tells about practices of science. One practice is to observe things and tell about them. Hold up an object, and ask your child to tell something about it. Then reverse roles with your child.

Inquiry **Try It!**

How do we observe?

4 Draw.

myscienceonline.com

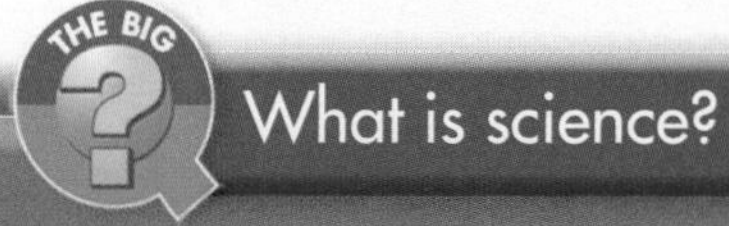

Name ______________________________

Try It!

How do we observe?

Draw.

Directions: Have children observe an object with a hand lens and draw what they see.

Picture Clues

Look at the pictures.
What do you use
to measure?
What helps you
stay safe?

Name ____

Picture Clues

Circle what the girl can use to measure.

Circle what the boy can use to stay safe.

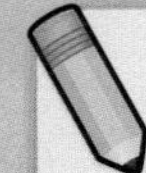

Directions: Ask children to put their finger on the picture of the girl. Have them name each object in the row and circle the object the girl can use to measure. Repeat the process with the picture of the boy, asking children to circle the object the boy can use to stay safe.

Home Activity: Look around your home with your child. Take turns finding things you use to measure and things you use to stay safe.

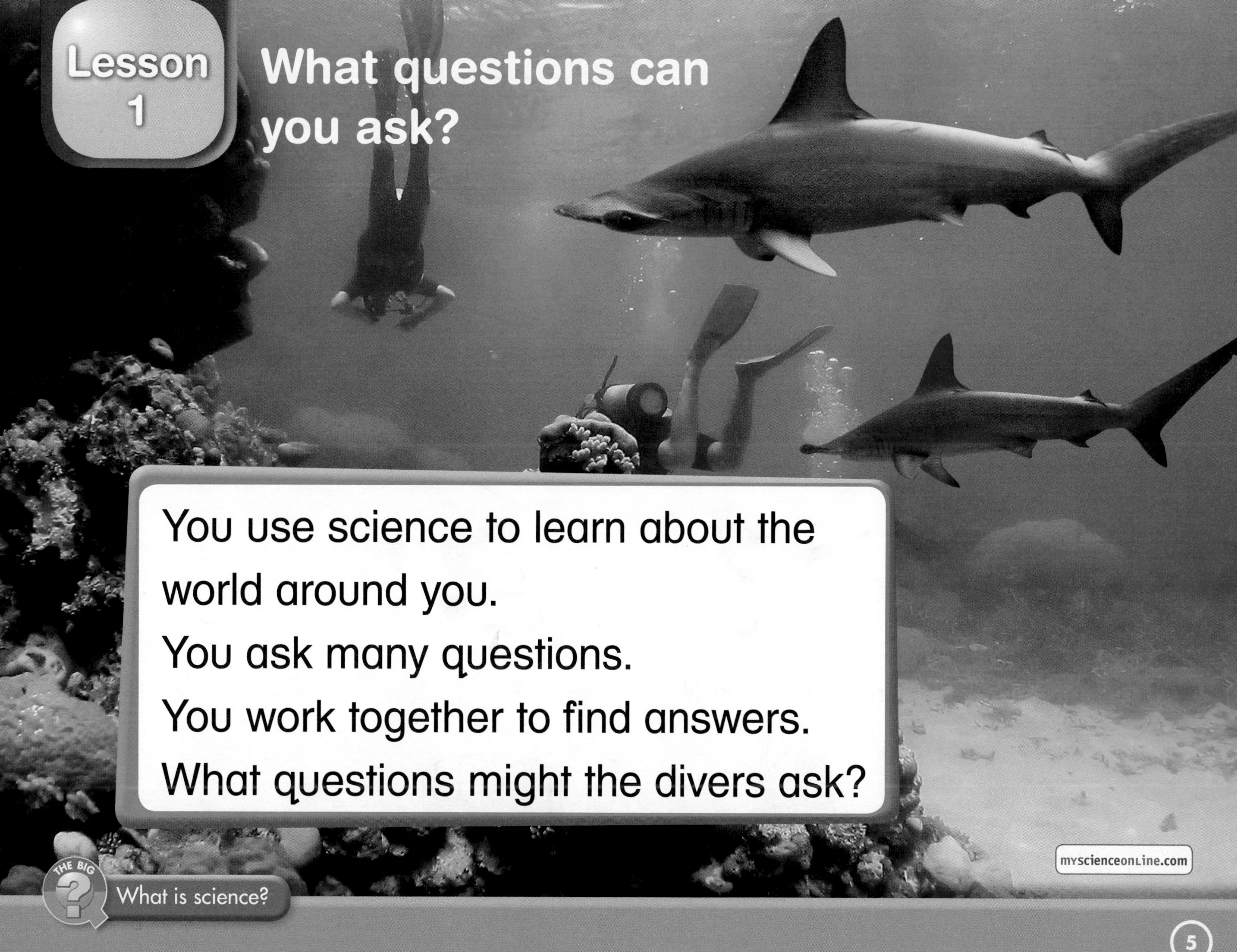

Lesson 1

What questions can you ask?

You use science to learn about the world around you.
You ask many questions.
You work together to find answers.
What questions might the divers ask?

The Big ? What is science?

myscienceonline.com

Lesson 1

Name ______________________________

What questions can you ask?

Circle the picture that answers each question.

Which object is heavy?

Which animal can fly?

Which object goes around and around?

Directions: Read aloud the first question to children. Help them identify the pictures in the row. Have children choose and circle the picture that best answers the question. Ask them to explain how they figured out the answer. Repeat with the other questions.

Home Activity: Take turns with your child, asking each other questions about objects in your home and answering them. After each question and answer, talk about what you did to figure out the answer.

How do you observe?

You observe the world.
You use your senses to observe.
You use your senses to look, hear, smell, touch, and taste.
These people are using their senses.
Tell what they observe.

mySCIENCEonLine.com

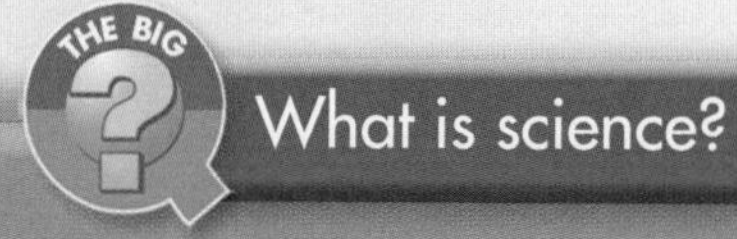

Name ______________________________

How do you observe?

Circle the pictures to answer the questions.

What can you observe by looking?

What can you observe by hearing?

What can you observe by touching?

Directions: Read aloud the first question to children. Help them identify the pictures in the row. Have children circle the object(s) that a person can observe by looking. Ask children to explain their choice(s). Repeat with the other questions. Point out that children may have to circle more than one object in a row.

Home Activity: Choose an object in your home. Ask your child how he or she can observe the object. If necessary, ask a question about each sense—looking, hearing, touching, smelling, and tasting—and let your child answer. For example, ask: "Can you touch the object?"

How do you learn together?

You share ideas with others.
You test your ideas.
You help each other do tests.
Together you learn new things.
These children want to learn what can soak up water best.

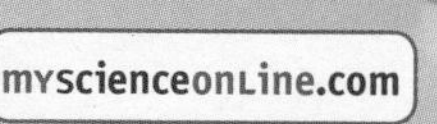

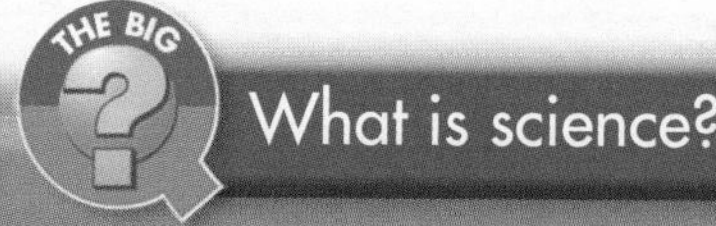

Lesson 3

Name ____________________

How do you learn together?

Color the picture that shows children working together.

Activity 7
Use with page 7.

Directions: Discuss the two pictures with children. Ask them what the children are doing and why. Then ask children which picture shows children working together. Have children color that picture.

Home Activity: Plan a task with your child, such as setting the table. First, talk about the task and decide how to divide the work. Then do the task. Afterward, talk about how planning and sharing helped with the work.

Lesson 4

How do you share what you learn?

You share what you learn.
You write and draw.
You talk and show pictures.

THE BIG ? What is science?

Lesson 4

Name ______________________________

How do you share what you learn?

Think of something that moves.

Share what you know about it.

Draw a picture of it.

Directions: Ask children to think of something that moves. It could be an animal, an object, or a person. Explain that children will share what they know about this topic with others by drawing a picture of it. Encourage them to include as many details as possible in their picture. Have children take turns displaying their pictures and telling about them.

Home Activity: Tell your child about something you learned today. Ask your child to tell you about something he or she learned in school today. Point out that you have both shared what you learned.

What do you use to observe?

You use tools to observe.
You use tools to measure.
You use tools to write and draw.
Tools help you learn.

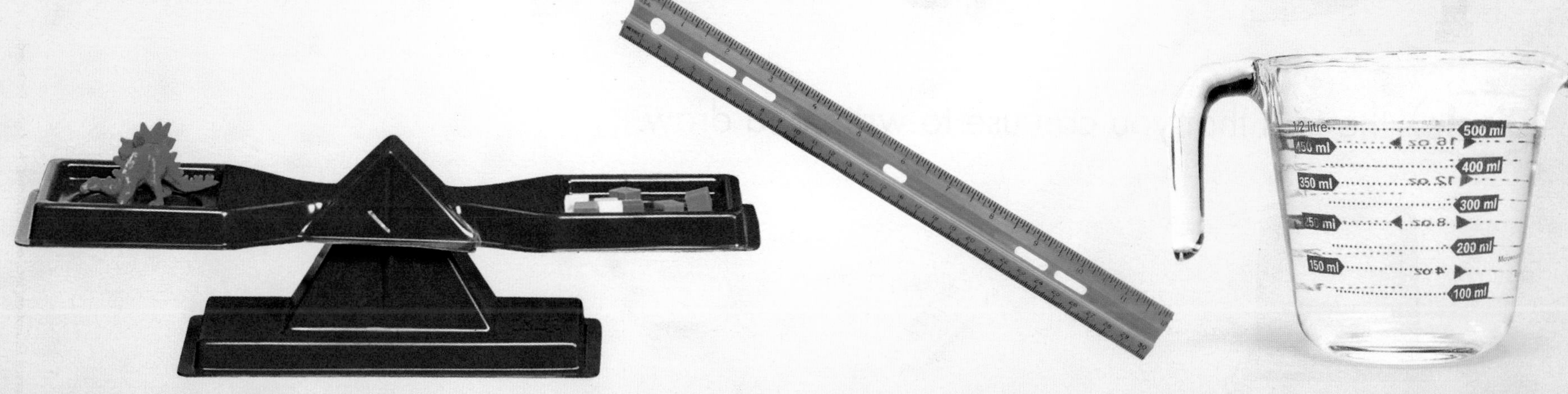

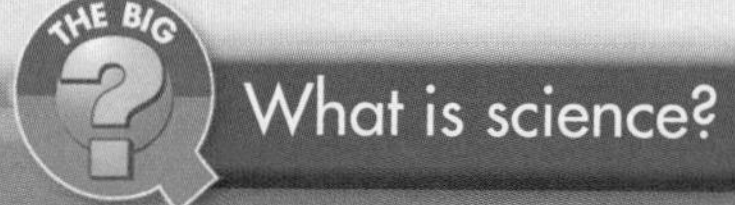

Lesson 5

Name ______________________________

What do you use to observe?

Circle the tool that you can use to look at things.

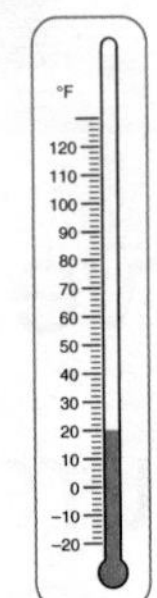

Circle the tool that you can use to measure.

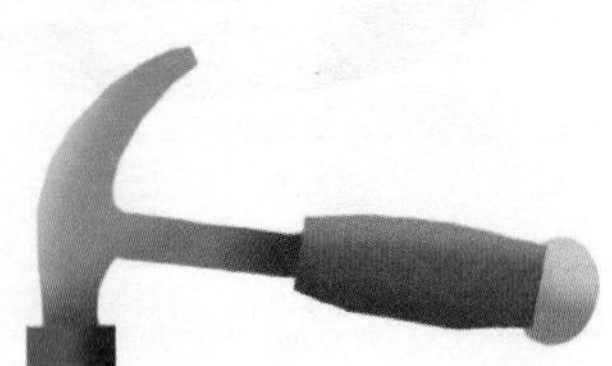

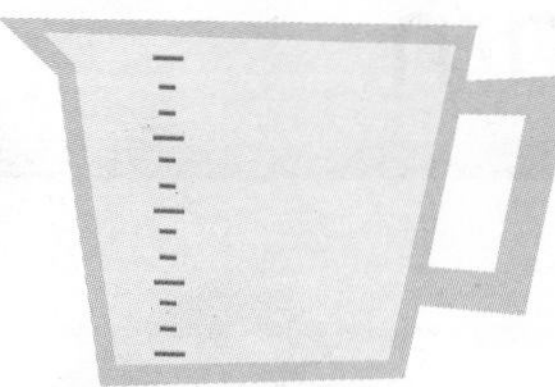

Circle the tool that you can use to write and draw.

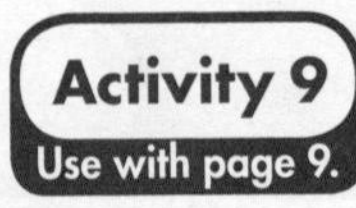

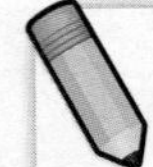

Directions: Read aloud the first direction to children. Help them identify the pictures in the row. Have children choose and circle the object that they can use to look at things. Ask children to explain their choice. Repeat with the other directions.

Home Activity: With your child, make lists of *Tools for Looking, Tools for Measuring,* and *Tools for Writing and Drawing*. Start with the tools on the page. Add other tools as you and your child think of them.

How do you stay safe?

Rules and tools can help keep you safe.

You follow safety rules in science.

What tools help you stay safe?

Safety Rules

1. Listen to your teacher.
2. Tie your hair back.
3. Use safety tools.
4. Handle all tools carefully.
5. Wear safety goggles.
6. Wash your hands.

mysciencEonLine.com

THE BIG ? What is science?

Lesson 6

Name ______________________________

How do you stay safe?

Circle the picture that shows a child following a science safety rule.

Activity 10
Use with page 10.

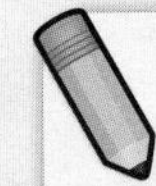

Directions: Remind children of science safety rules. Then read aloud the direction to children. Have children circle the picture showing a child following a science safety rule. Then discuss the rules depicted.

Home Activity: Talk with your child about safety rules in the home. Together make a list of rules and post the list where everyone can see it.

Inquiry Investigate It!

How do things look?

You need
journal
viewer
plastic cup with water
objects

1 Look.

Draw.

2 Pour.

3 Look

Draw.

myscienceonLine.com

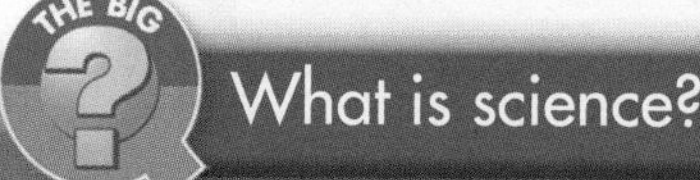

Name ______________________________

Inquiry **Investigate It!**

How do things look?

Draw.

How Things Look	
No Water	**Through Water**

Activity 11
Use with page 11.

Directions: Have children observe an object outside the viewer and then inside the viewer. Have children compare the two views.

Science Careers

Student Inventor

Inventors observe their world.
Inventors make things for the first time.
Christen Wooley is an inventor.
Christen was twelve years old
when she invented a backpack vest.

myscienceonline.com

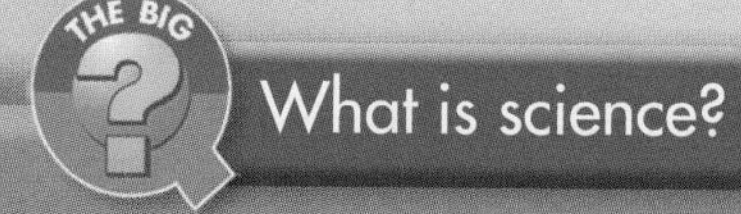

Name ______________________________

Student Inventor

Circle things you could carry in a backpack vest.

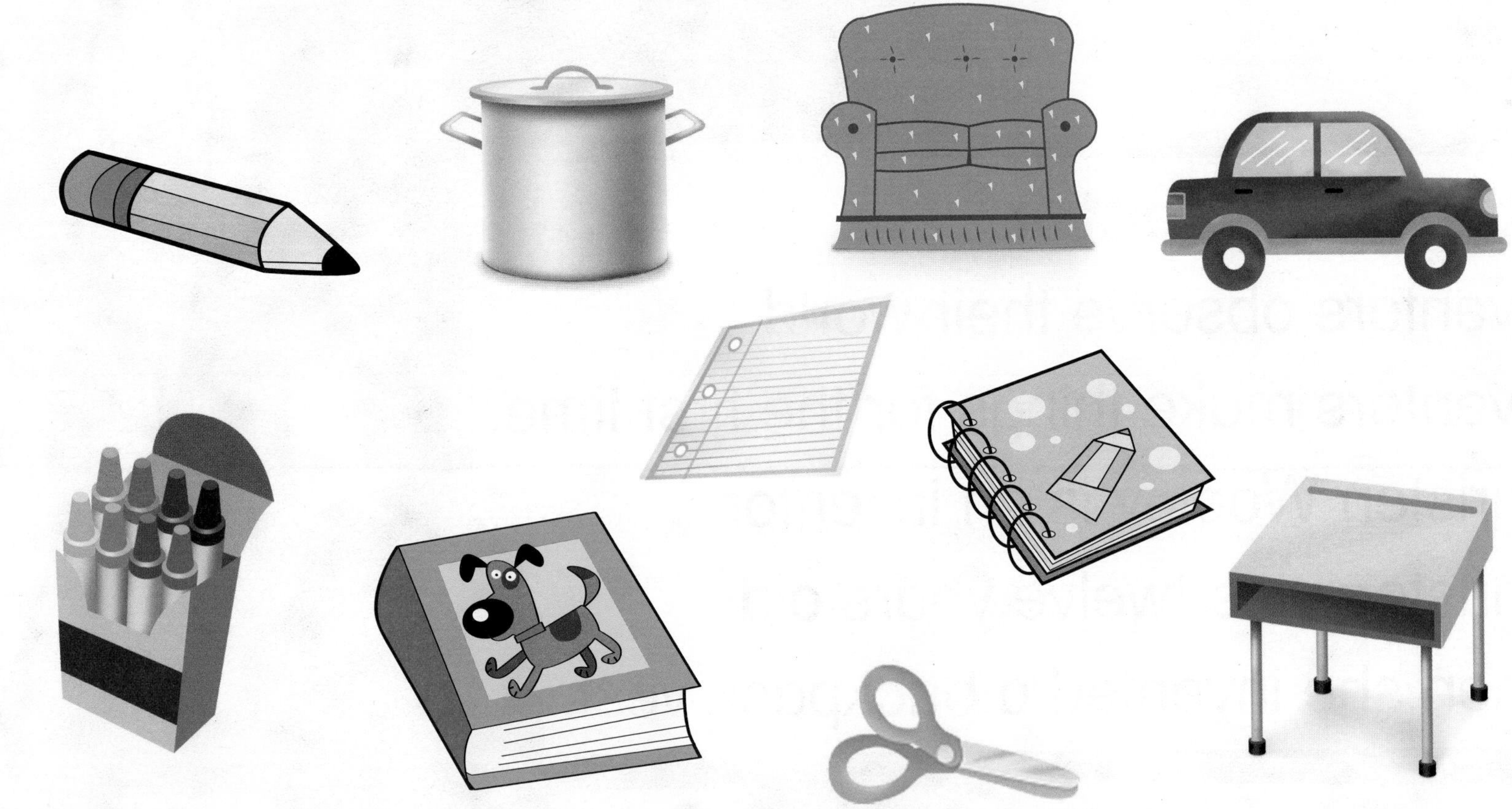

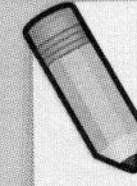

Directions: Review Christen Wooley's invention with children. Discuss how the vest can be used to carry things to and from school. Talk about the kinds of things children put in backpacks. Explain that they could put the same things in the backpack vest. Then have children circle objects they could carry in it.

Home Activity: Play a game of "put it in the backpack" with your child. Point to an object and ask your child if you can put it into a backpack. Anything can go in the backpack if it can fit inside and is not too heavy. Your child should say no to a chair but yes to a small stuffed animal, for example.

Solve Problems

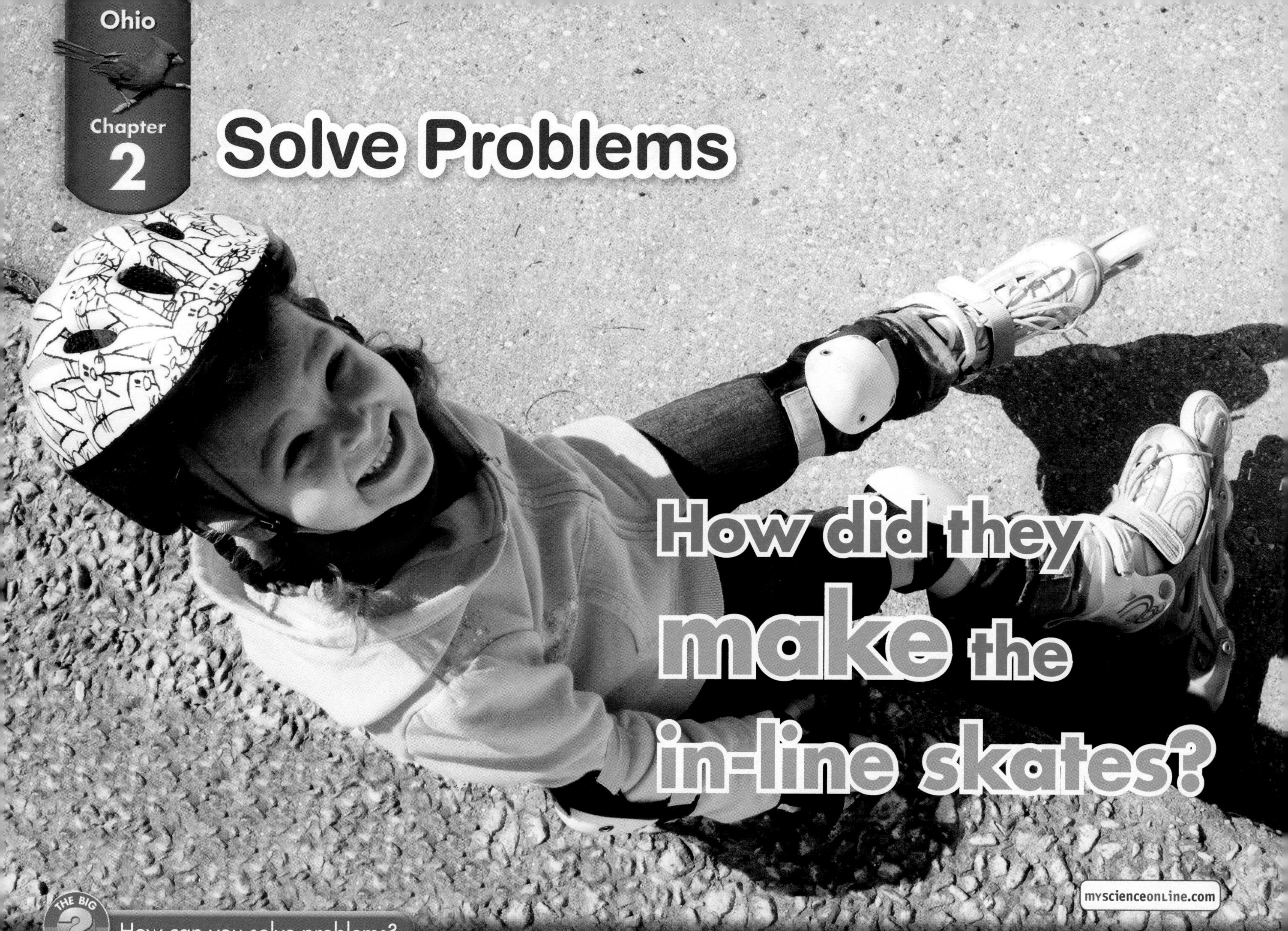

How did they make the in-line skates?

How can you solve problems?

Ohio

Name ____________________

How can you solve problems?

Circle the picture that shows in-line skates.

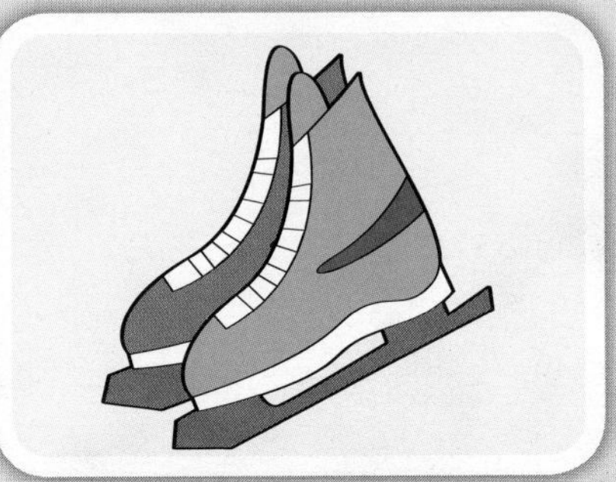

Draw a picture of someone skating with in-line skates.

Activity 13
Use with page 13.

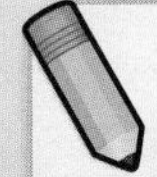
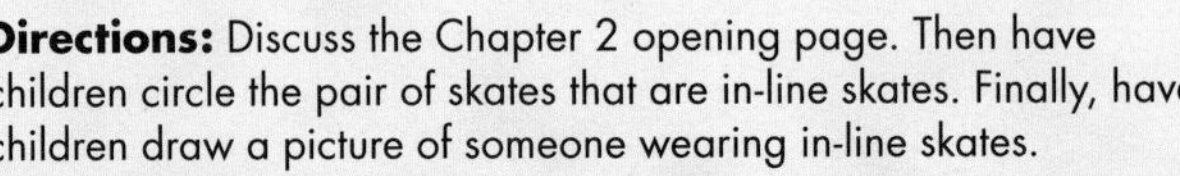
Directions: Discuss the Chapter 2 opening page. Then have children circle the pair of skates that are in-line skates. Finally, have children draw a picture of someone wearing in-line skates.

Home Activity: Your child is studying science and technology. Show your child pictures of old and new technologies, such as telephones, cameras, and music players.

What can this object do?

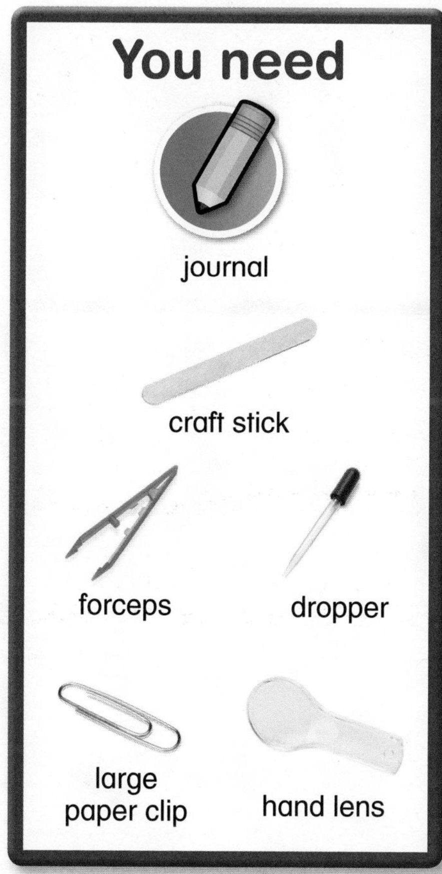

You need
journal
craft stick
forceps
dropper
large paper clip
hand lens

1. Look.
2. Choose.
   Draw.
3. Tell.
4. Compare.

myscienceonline.com

How can you solve problems?

Name ______________________________

Inquiry Try It!

What can this object do?

Choose.

Draw.

Activity 14
Use with page 14.

Directions: Have children use the hand lens to look at the forceps, dropper, craft stick, and paper clip. Then have children draw what they see.

Let's Read Science!

Cause and Effect

What made the light turn on?

THE BIG ? How can you solve problems?

mySCIENCEonLine.com

Name ____

Cause and Effect

Look at what happened in each row.

Circle the picture that shows why it happened.

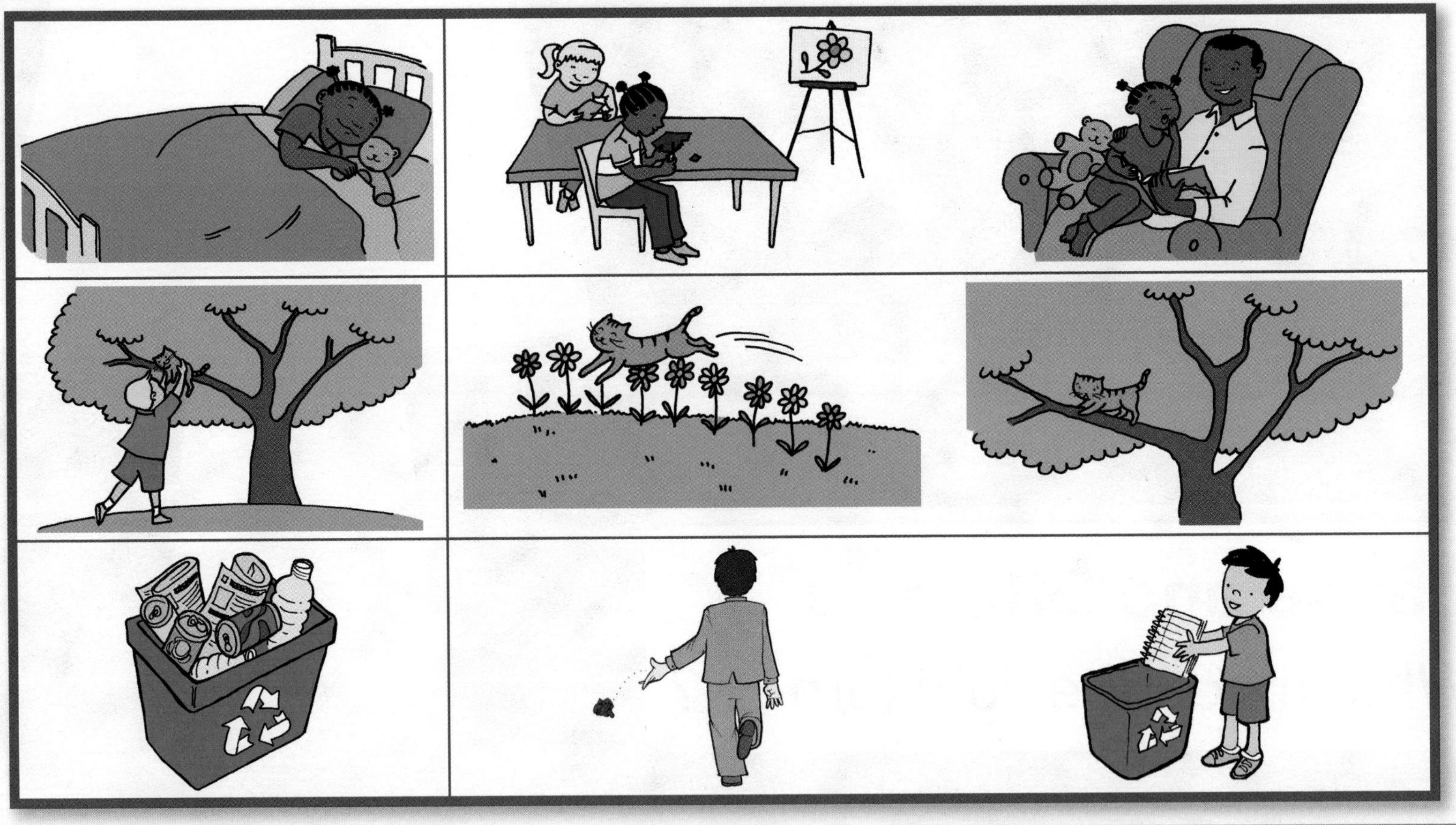

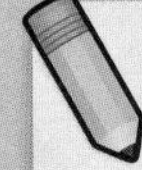

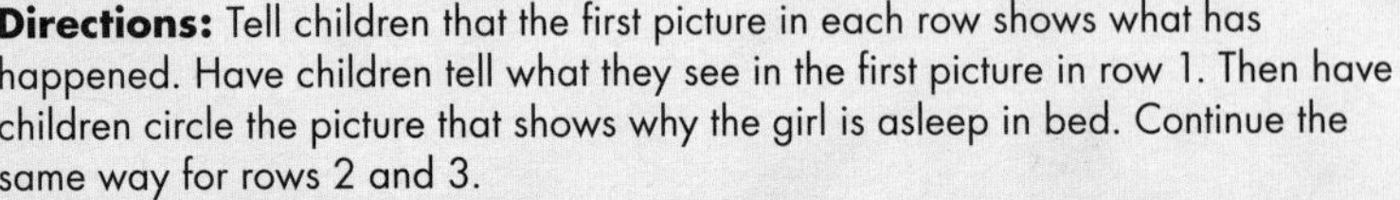

Directions: Tell children that the first picture in each row shows what has happened. Have children tell what they see in the first picture in row 1. Then have children circle the picture that shows why the girl is asleep in bed. Continue the same way for rows 2 and 3.

Home Activity: Help children point out cause-and-effect relationships in their everyday lives. For example, your teeth are clean and healthy because you brush them.

Lesson 1 What problem can you solve?

You might spill when you drink from a glass.
This is a problem.
A straw is the solution.
Many straws are plastic.

THE BIG ? How can you solve problems?

Lesson 1

Name ______________________________

What problem can you solve?

Look at the problem in the first picture.

Circle a solution to the problem.

Activity 16
Use with page 16.

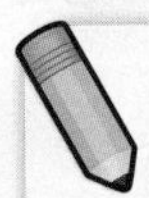

Directions: Help children identify the problem shown in the first picture in the first row. Ask them to circle a possible solution to the problem. Repeat the procedure for the second row.

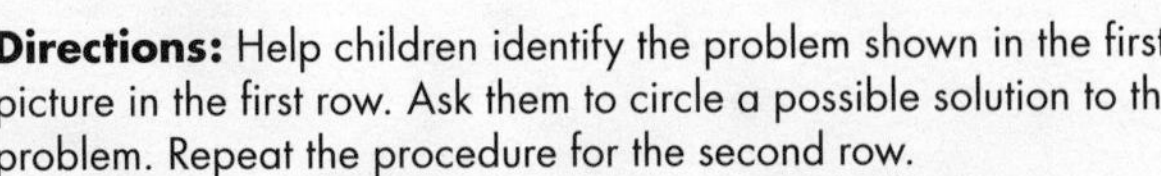

Home Activity: Identify simple household problems, such as dirty dishes or dry plants. Ask your child to help you identify a way to solve the problem and then help you carry out the solution.

Lesson 2

How can you make a plan?

You plan how to make a straw.
You write and draw.
You make the straw.
It works!

THE BIG ? How can you solve problems?

Lesson 2

Name ______________________________

How can you make a plan?

Think of a something you would like to make with connecting blocks.

 **Draw** a plan. Show what you want to make.

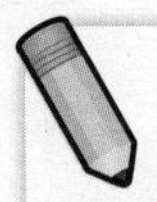 **Directions:** Tell children that a plan shows what to make or how to make it. Then tell children to draw something they could make with connecting blocks. Encourage them to use the blocks to make what their plans show.

 **Home Activity:** Talk with your child about plans you use or make. You may use recipes in the kitchen or draw up a list of errands. You may follow plans for putting together a toy or piece of furniture. Show the plans to your child and tell how you use them.

Lesson 3 How can you share your ideas with others?

You show your drawing.
You tell about the straw.
Others can use the straw too.

THE BIG ? How can you solve problems?

Name ______________________________

How can you share your ideas with others?

Circle the picture of a person sharing information.

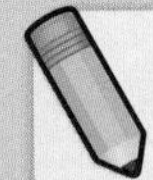

Directions: Discuss with children how they can share ideas and information with others. Then have children circle the picture showing someone sharing information.

Home Activity: Draw a picture of something you plan to do tomorrow, such as walk your child to school or make dinner. Share your picture with your child and discuss what it shows.

Inquiry **Investigate It!**

How can you lift heavy things?

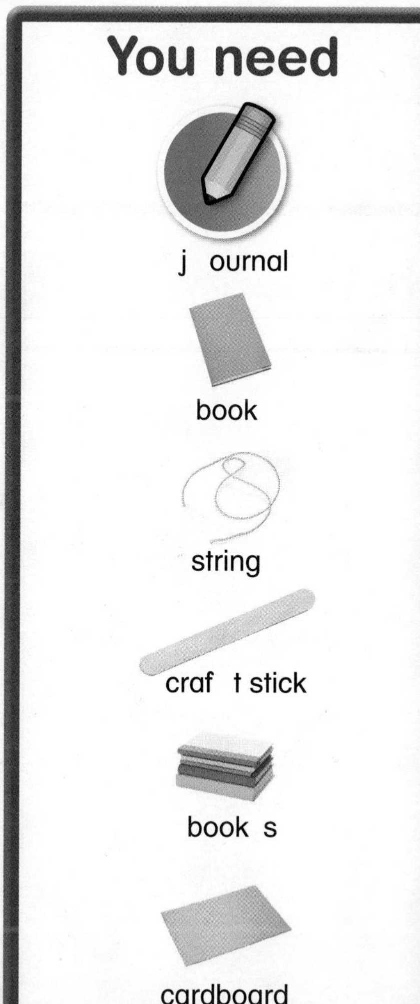

1 Tie.

2 Put.

3 Pull.

4 Put.

5 Push.

6 Write.

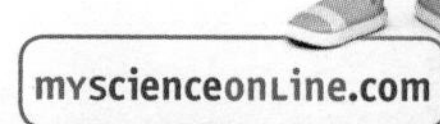

Name ____

Inquiry **Investigate It!**

How can you lift heavy things?

Draw.

Pull	Push

Activity 19
Use with page 19.

Directions: Have children draw how they pull the book up the ramp and how they push the book up the ramp.

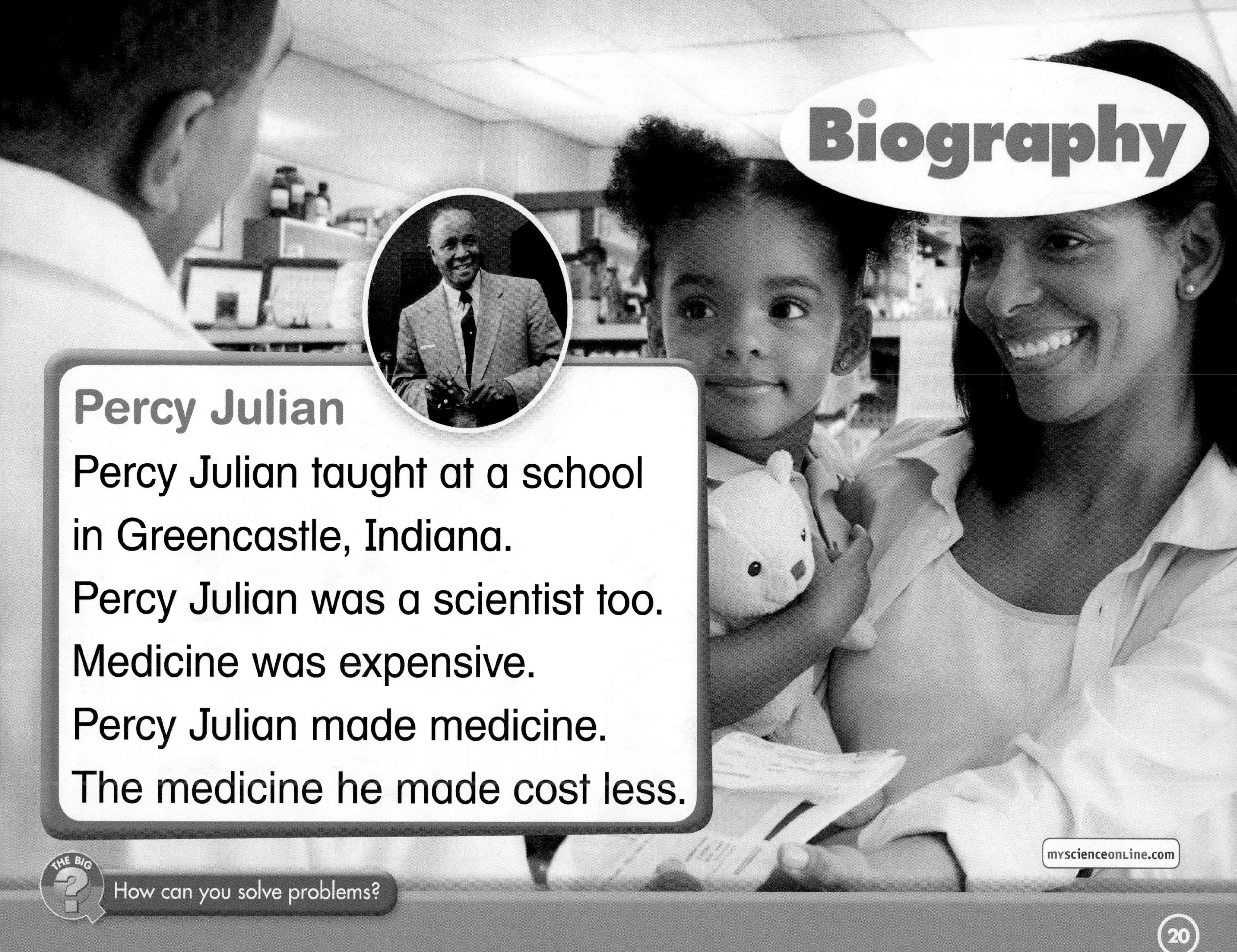

Biography

Percy Julian

Percy Julian taught at a school in Greencastle, Indiana.

Percy Julian was a scientist too.

Medicine was expensive.

Percy Julian made medicine.

The medicine he made cost less.

myscienceonLine.com

THE BIG ? How can you solve problems?

Name ___________________________________

Percy Julian

Circle the pictures that show tools Percy Julian would have used in his science lab.

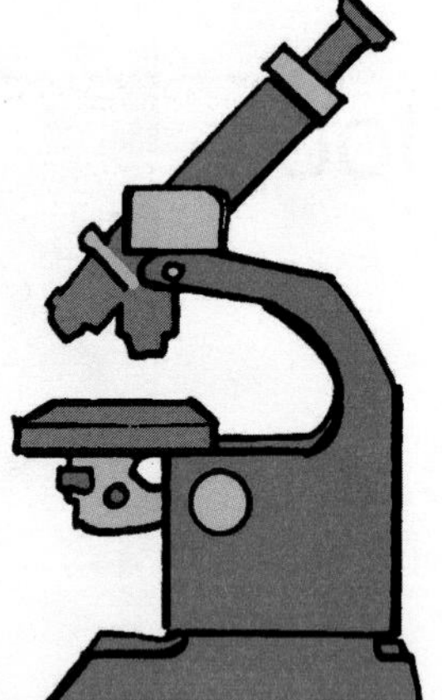

Directions: Remind children that Percy Julian was a scientist. Help them recall the tools a scientist uses. Then ask them to circle the tools Percy Julian might have used in his work as a scientist.

Home Activity: Your child learned about Percy Julian, a teacher and scientist. Ask your child to tell you about the tools scientists use in their work.

Inquiry **Design It!**

How can you make a maze?

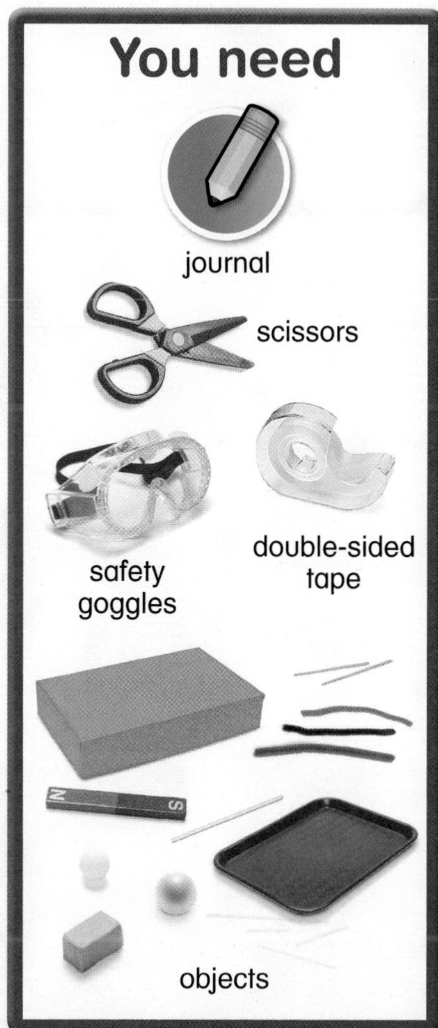

You need
journal
scissors
safety goggles
double-sided tape
objects

1 Plan.

2 Draw.

3 Make.

4 Test.

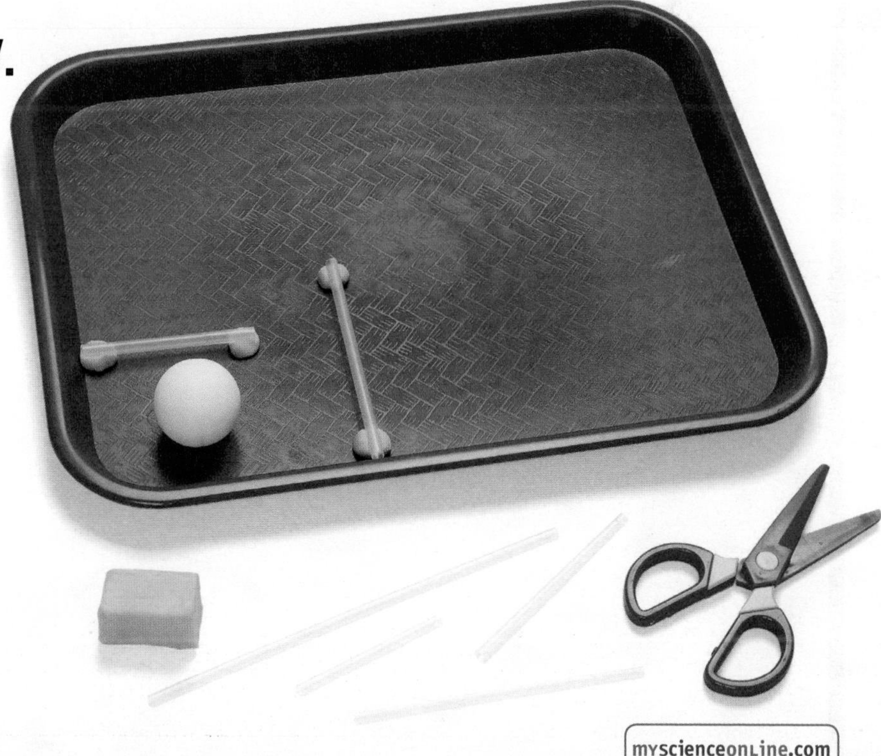

myscienceonline.com

How can you solve problems?

Name ____________________

Inquiry **Design It!**

How can you make a maze?

Draw.

Activity 21
Use with page 21.

Directions: Have children draw their maze before they begin to make it.

Ohio

Unit B

Life Science

Chapter 3

Living and Nonliving Things

THE BIG ? What can you tell about living things?

Chipmunks store food in their big cheeks.

Name ______________________________

Life Science

Draw a plant.

Draw an animal.

Directions: Discuss plants and animals, asking children to name different kinds of plants and animals. Then have children draw a plant and an animal. Have them tell about the plant and the animal they drew.

Home Activity: In science, your child is learning about living things. Together with your child, look through a picture book and ask your child to point to living things and identify them as plants or animals.

Living and Nonliving Things

Which is living?

What can you tell about living things?

myscienceonLine.com

Ohio

Name ______________________________

What can you tell about living things?

Look at the bears.

Circle two bears that look like living bears.

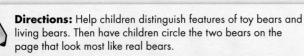

Directions: Help children distinguish features of toy bears and living bears. Then have children circle the two bears on the page that look most like real bears.

Home Activity: With your child, gather and sort pictures of living animals and toy or cartoon animals. Talk about how you can tell the difference between the real animals and the toy or cartoon animals.

What things are living?

1 Look.

2 Tell.

3 Draw.

Name ______________________________

Try It!

What things are living?

Circle two living things.

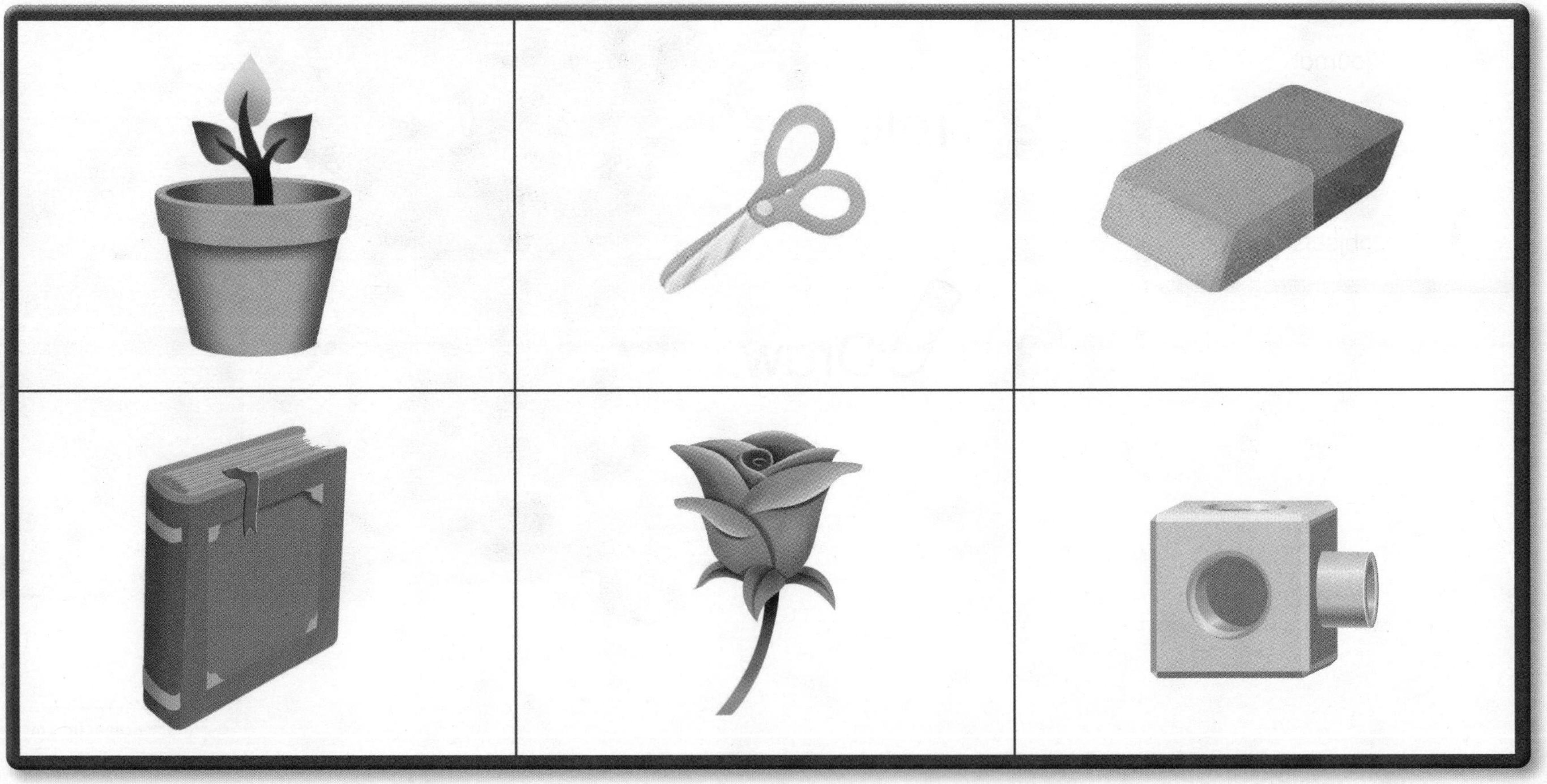

Directions: Have children circle the pictures of two living things.

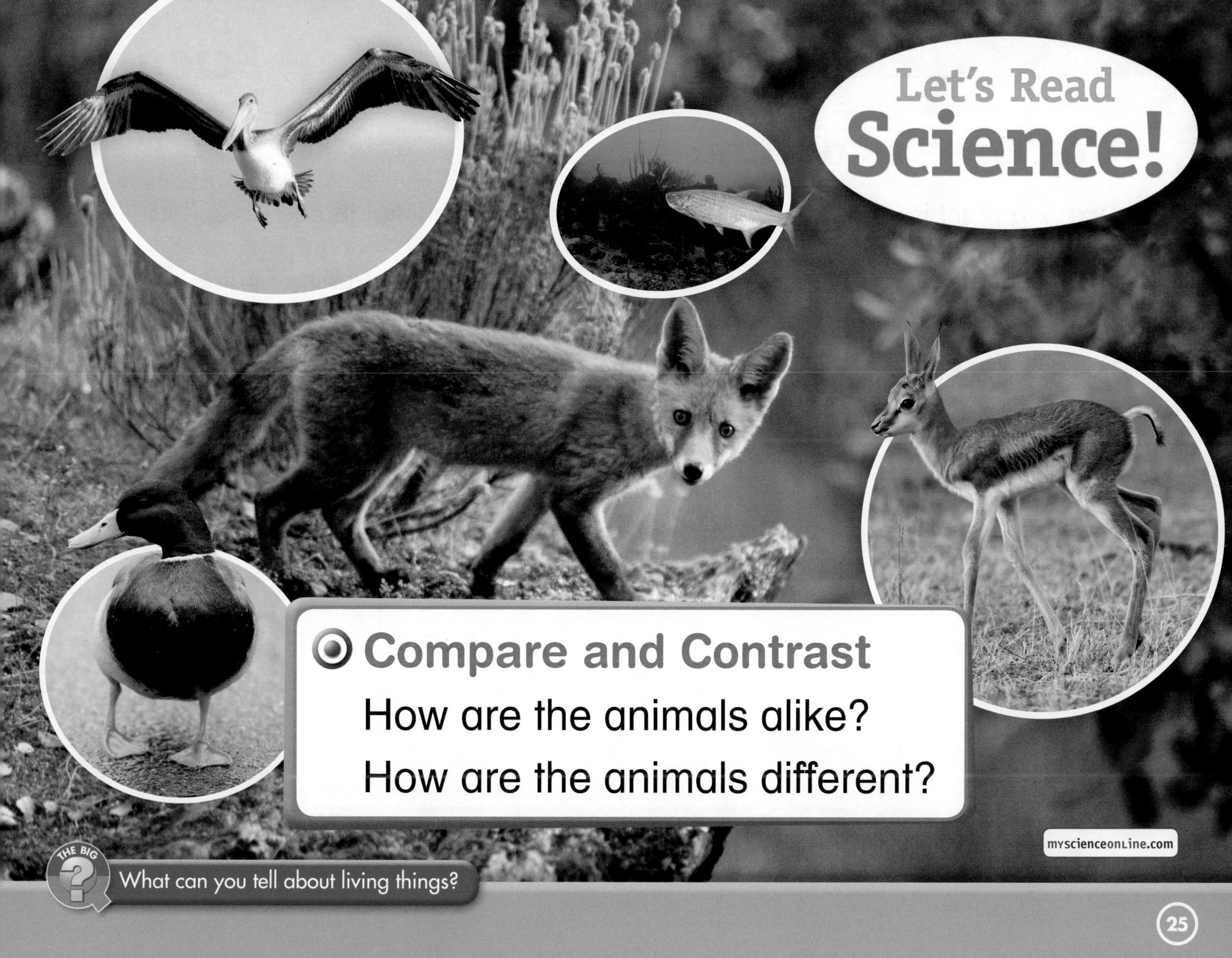
Let's Read
Science!
Compare and Contrast
How are the animals alike?
How are the animals different?
myscienceonline.com
THE BIG ?
What can you tell about living things?

Name ____

Compare and Contrast

Draw a plant in one box.

Draw a different plant in the other box.

Tell how the two plants are alike.

Draw an animal in one box.

Draw a different animal in the other box.

Tell how the two animals are alike.

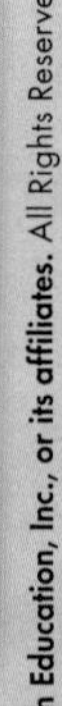

Directions: Have children think of two plants they can draw. Offer suggestions or show pictures, if necessary. When children have finished drawing, have them tell how their two plants are alike and different. Repeat with two animals.

Home Activity: Show your child pictures of two different kinds of plants. Take turns telling how the plants are alike and different.

Lesson 1 What are living things?

Living things grow.

Living things change or move on their own.

Plants and animals are living things.

You are a living thing too.

Look around.

You will see many living things.

myscienceonline.com

THE BIG ? What can you tell about living things?

Lesson 1

Name ______________________________

What are living things?

Circle the two living things in the picture.

Color the picture.

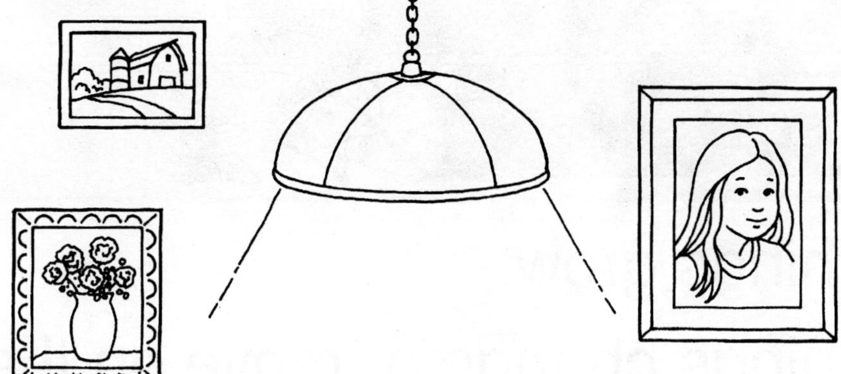

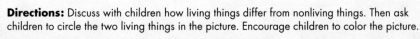

Directions: Discuss with children how living things differ from nonliving things. Then ask children to circle the two living things in the picture. Encourage children to color the picture.

Home Activity: Help your child identify living things in and around your home.

Lesson 2 What do living things need?

All living things have needs.
Living things need space and air.
Living things need water and food.
You are a living thing.
What do you need?

myscienceonline.com

THE BIG ? What can you tell about living things?

Lesson 2

Name ______________________________

What do living things need?

Color the picture of the boy meeting a need.

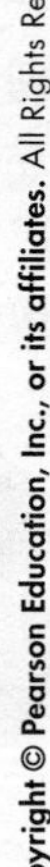

Activity 27
Use with page 27.

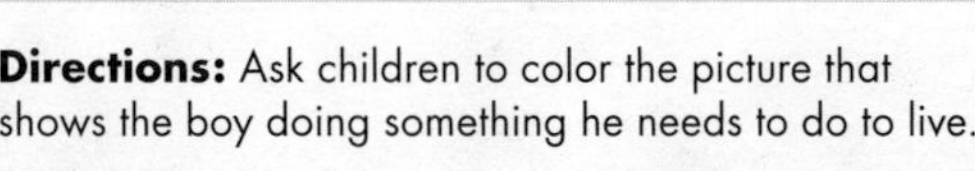
Directions: Ask children to color the picture that shows the boy doing something he needs to do to live.

Home Activity: Let your child help you water a plant, feed a pet, or pour a glass of juice. Talk about how living things need food, water, air, and space to live.

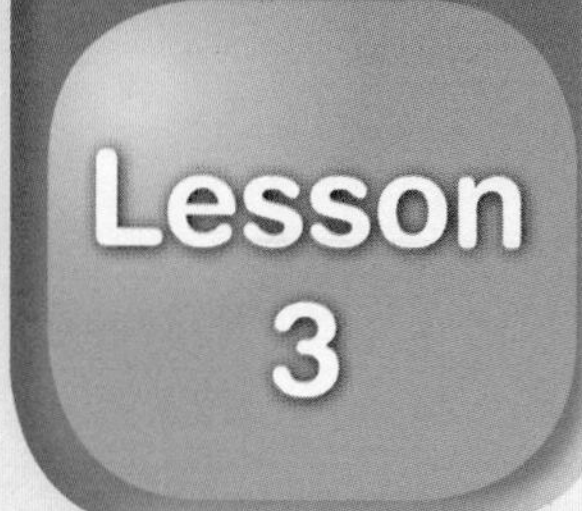

How are animals alike and different?

Animals have different colors and shapes.
Animals have different body coverings.
Animals have different ways of moving.
Tell about the animals in the pictures.
How are they alike?

THE BIG ? What can you tell about living things?

Lesson 3

Name ______________________________

How are animals alike and different?

Circle the two animals that move alike.

Circle the animal that has fur or hair.

Circle the animal that does not have legs.

Directions: Help children identify the pictures in the first row. Repeat the process for the pictures in the second and third rows.

Home Activity: Identify features of animals you and your child see. For example, if you see a dog, note that it moves by walking and running, its body is covered with fur, and so on.

Lesson 4

How are plants alike and different?

Plants can be different shapes, sizes, and colors. Plants can feel rough or smooth. Tell about the plants in the picture. Tell how they might feel.

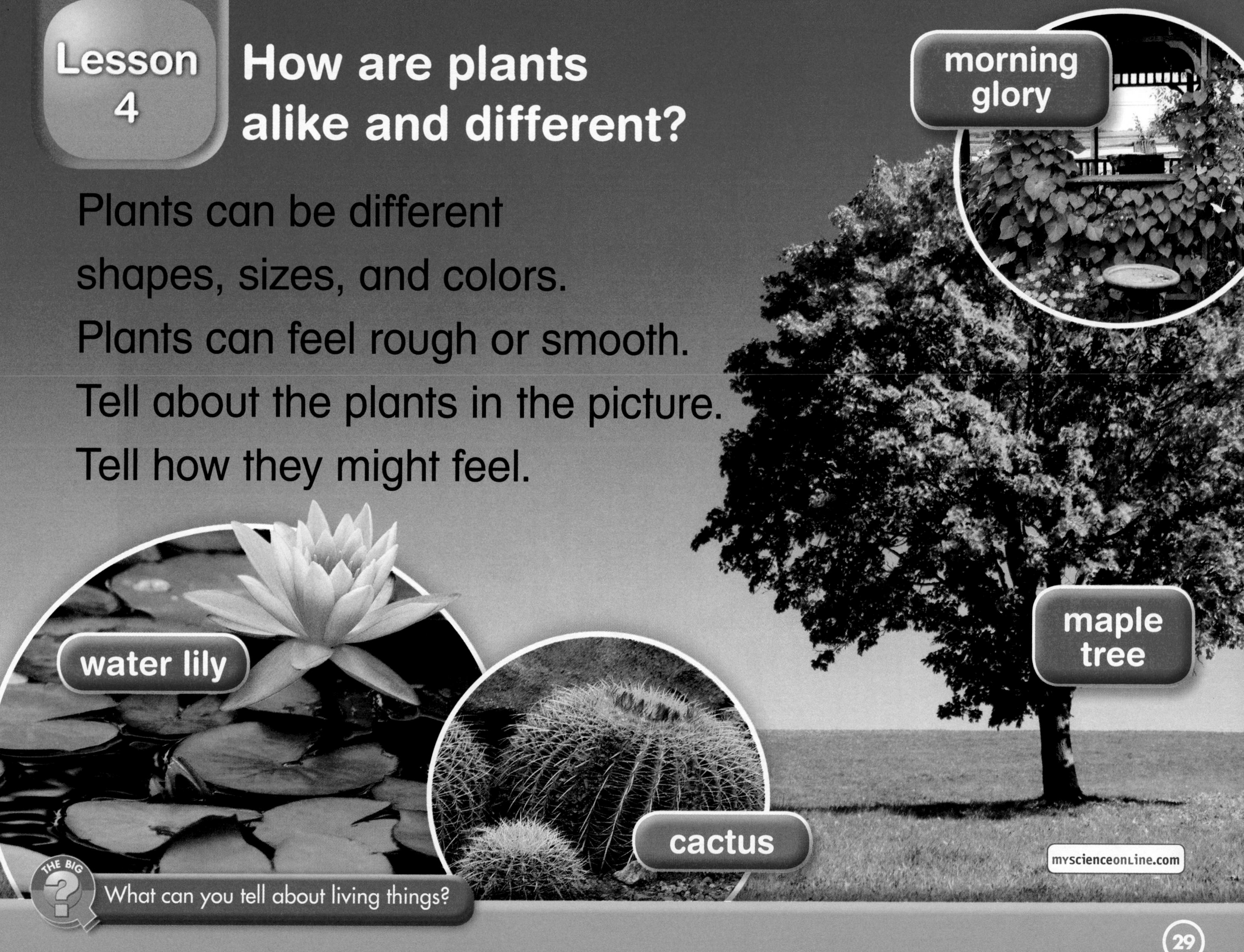

THE BIG ? What can you tell about living things?

Lesson 4

Name ______________________________

How are plants alike and different?

Color the tree trunk and branch brown.

Color leaves green.

Color the flower red.

Draw an X on a plant part that feels rough.

Circle a plant part that feels smooth.

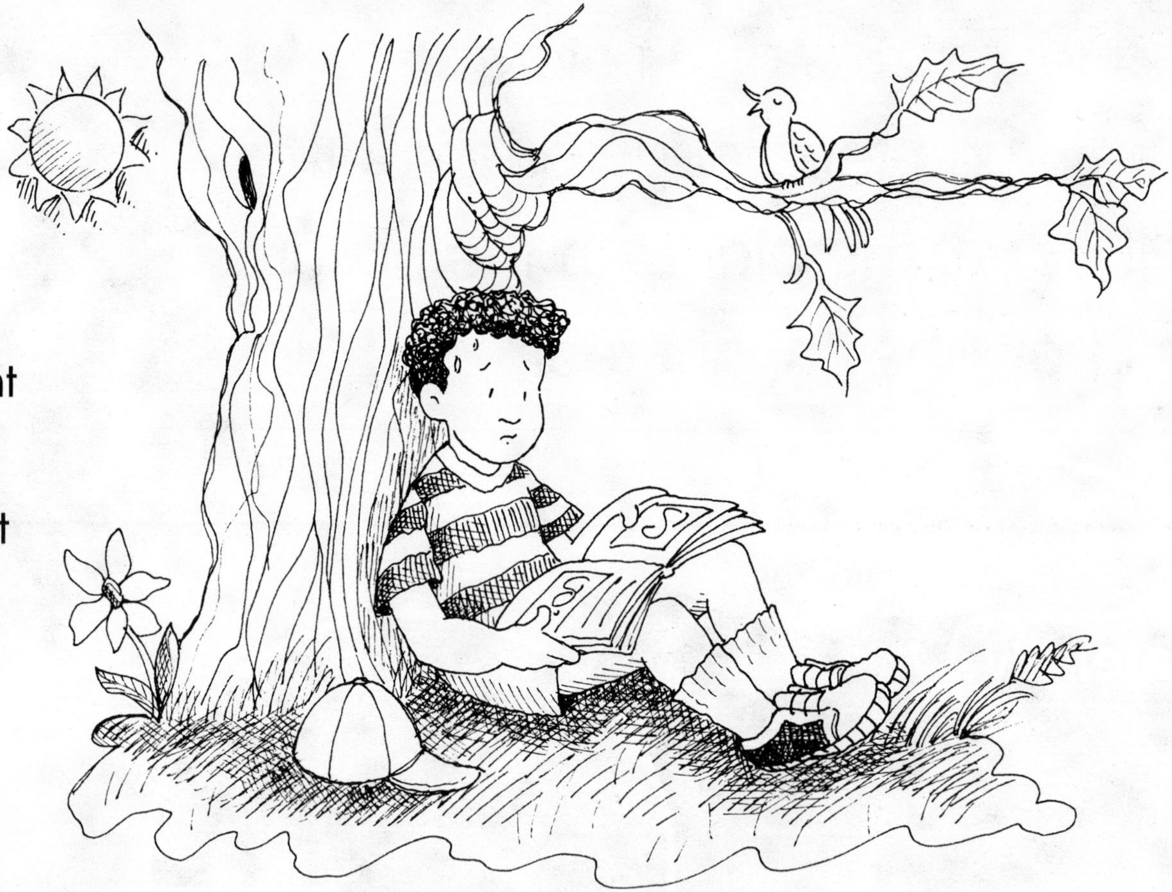

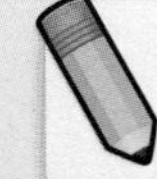

Directions: Read the directions to children and have them color the parts of the picture as directed. Then have them draw an X on a rough plant part and circle a smooth plant part.

Home Activity: If possible, feel plant parts with your child and talk about the textures. Tree trunks may feel rough whereas flowers may feel smooth.

Investigate It!

How are animals and plants different?

1. Look.
2. Write.
3. Compare.
4. Tell.

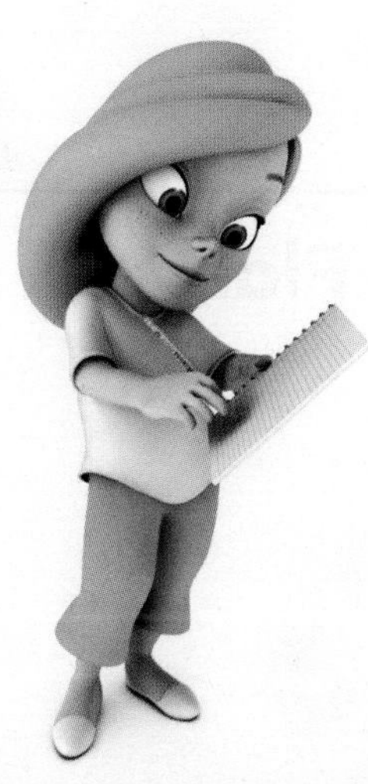

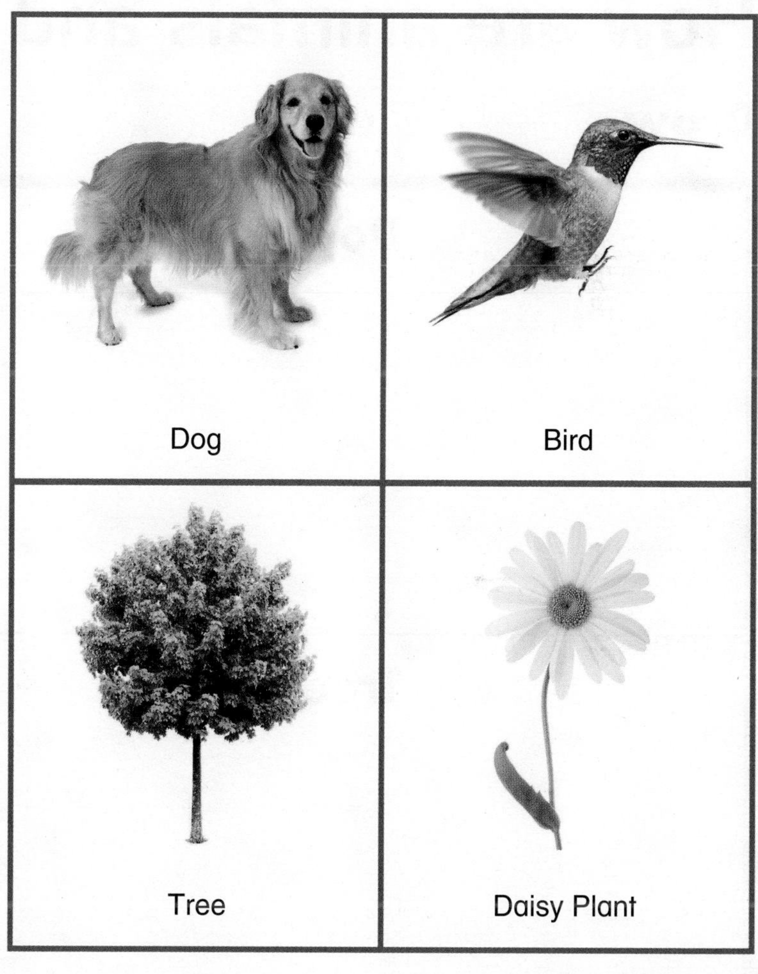

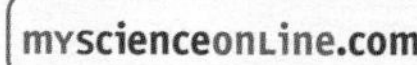

Name ____________________

Investigate It!

How are animals and plants different?

Draw.

Dog	Bird
Tree	Daisy Plant

Activity 30
Use with page 30.

Directions: Have children look at the images of the dog, bird, tree, and daisy plant in the Investigate It activity. Then have children draw pictures that show the features of each living thing.

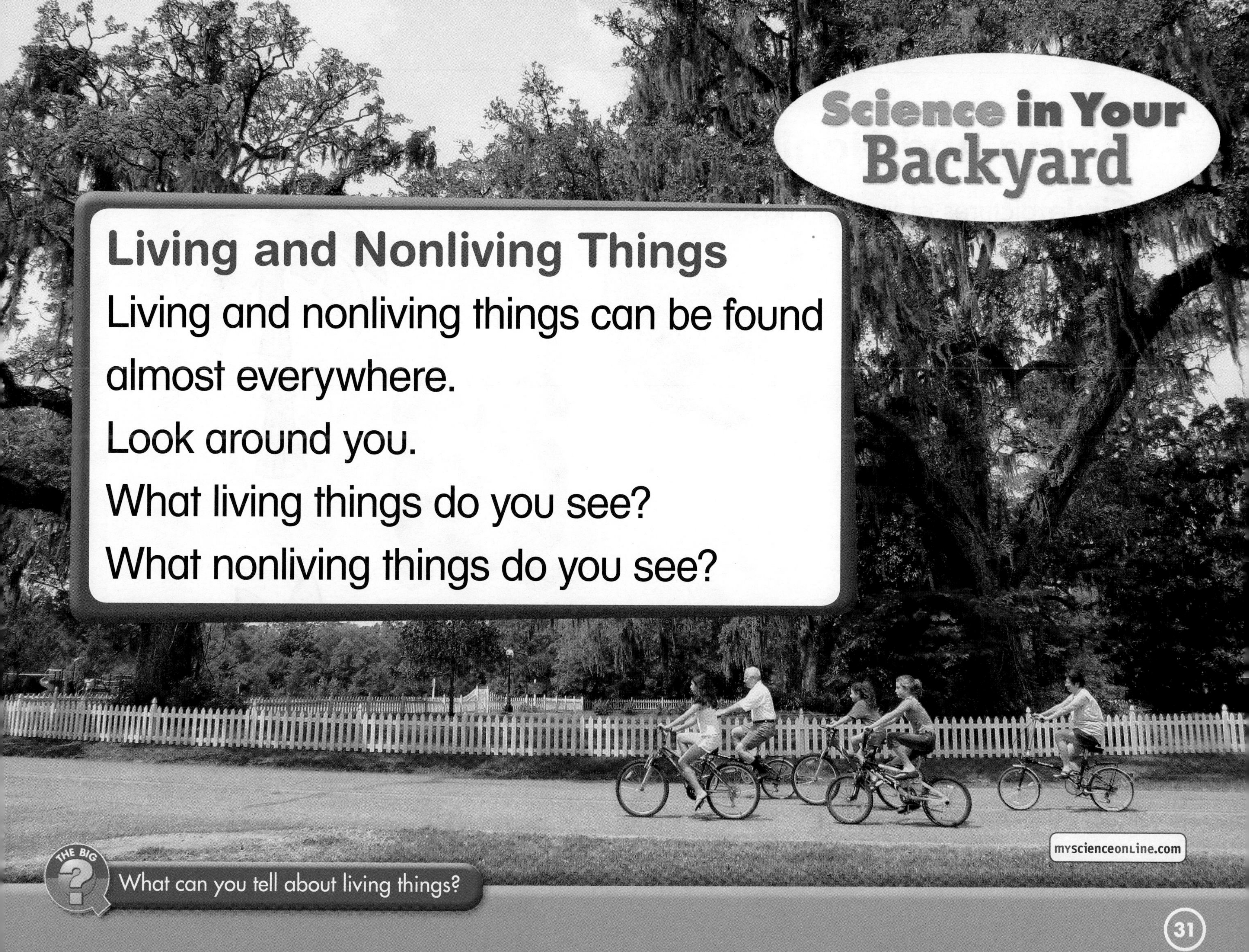

Living and Nonliving Things

Living and nonliving things can be found almost everywhere.

Look around you.

What living things do you see?

What nonliving things do you see?

THE BIG ? What can you tell about living things?

myscienceonLine.com

Name ______________________________

Living and Nonliving Things

Circle pictures of living things.

Directions: Identify each picture in the box. Then have children circle the pictures of living things.

Home Activity: As you walk with your child, take turns identifying living and nonliving things.

Ohio
Unit
C
Earth Science
Chapter 4
Earth and Sky
THE BIG ?
What are Earth and the sky like?
The weather is usually warm in summer.

Name ____________________

Earth Science

Draw the sky.

Show the sun.

Directions: Tell children that in science you learn about the world around you. You can learn about the sky. Have children look out a classroom window at the sky, or take them outside to look at the sky. Remind them not to look directly at the sun. Ask them to draw a daytime sky with the sun in it. Encourage them to add something else they might see in the daytime sky.

Home Activity: Your child is learning about the sky, the seasons, and weather. With your child, look in picture books or magazines for pictures of the sky. Talk about what you see in the sky in each picture.

Ohio

Chapter 4

Earth and Sky

Is it night or day?

What are Earth and the sky like?

mySCIENCEonLine.com

Name ________________________________

What are Earth and sky like?

Look at the pictures.

Color the picture that shows what the chapter is about.

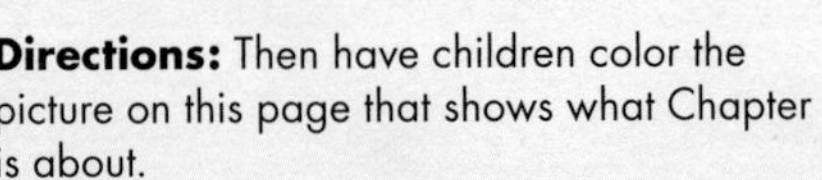

Directions: Then have children color the picture on this page that shows what Chapter 5 is about.

Home Activity: In Chapter 5, your child will learn about the sky and the objects that can be seen in the sky. Take time to look at the daytime sky with your child. Talk about what you see. Do you see clouds, the sun, airplanes, or birds?

Inquiry **Try It!**

How does weather change?

1 Observe the weather.

2 Record.

3 Count.

	Monday	Tuesday	Wednesday	Thursday	Friday
Clear					
Cloudy					
Partly cloudy					
Windy					
Rainy or snowy					
Foggy					

myscienceonLine.com

Name ____________________

Inquiry **Try It!**

How does weather change?

Record.

	Monday	Tuesday	Wednesday	Thursday	Friday
Clear					
Cloudy					
Partly Cloudy					
Rainy or snowy					
Windy					
Foggy					

Directions: Have children check the box for the type of weather they see each day. Have them record the weather each week for one month.

Let's Read Science!
Draw Conclusions
What was the weather like here?
How do you know?
myscienceonline.com
THE BIG ?
What are Earth and the sky like?

Name ______________________________

Draw Conclusions

Look at the picture of a place on Earth.

Circle the picture that tells what the weather is usually like in this place.

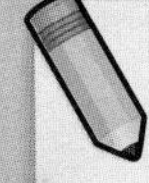

Directions: Discuss the place shown in the large picture. Then ask children to use what they know and the picture to draw conclusions about the weather in this place. Have children circle the small picture that shows what the weather is like.

Home Activity: Help your child practice drawing conclusions using weather-specific clothing, such as raincoats, mittens, shorts, umbrellas, and sweaters. Display the clothing and ask your child when he or she would wear it and why.

Lesson 1 What can you see in the day sky?

You can see clouds and the sun in the day sky.
Sometimes you can see the moon in the day sky.
Tell about objects in the day sky.

mysciencEonLine.com

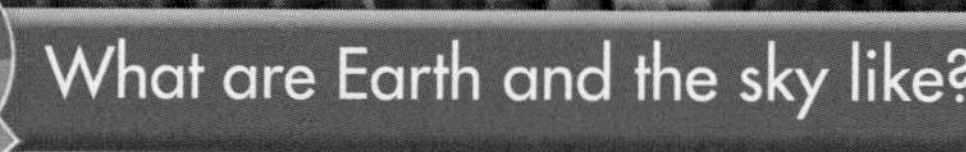

THE BIG ?
What are Earth and the sky like?

Lesson 1 Name ______________________________

What can you see in the day sky?

Circle the objects you might see in the day sky.

Directions: Have children identify each picture. Then have children circle the objects they can see in the sky during the day. Review the page, emphasizing that sometimes the moon can be seen in the day sky and sometimes it can be seen in the night sky. Ask which object is never seen in the sky.

Home Activity: Your child identified things that can be seen in the daytime sky. Together with your child, discuss what you would see in the daytime sky. Then draw a picture of the objects in the sky.

Lesson 2

How does the sun seem to move?

The sun looks low in the morning sky.
The sun looks high in the sky at noon.
The sun looks low in the evening sky.

noon

evening

morning

myscienceonline.com

THE BIG ? What are Earth and the sky like?

Lesson 2

Name ____________________

How does the sun seem to move?

Draw the sun. Show the sun in the early morning sky.

Draw the sun. Show the sun in the sky at noon.

Draw the sun. Show the sun in the early evening sky.

Activity 37

Use with page 37.

Directions: Read the directions for the first picture to children. Help them identify where to draw the sun. Then have them draw the sun. Repeat the process for the second and third pictures.

Home Activity: Together with your child look at the sky at different times of day. Draw pictures showing where the sun is at each time. Write the time on each picture.

Lesson 3

What can you see in the night sky?

You can see stars in the night sky. Sometimes you can see the moon in the night sky.

Sometimes you can see clouds too. Tell how objects in the day and night sky are alike.

THE BIG ? What are Earth and the sky like?

Lesson 3

Name ______________________________

What can you see in the night sky?

Circle the objects you might see in the night sky.

Draw a picture of the night sky.

Show the objects you circled.

Directions: Ask children to identify each picture and to circle the objects that can be seen in the night sky. Then have children draw a picture of the night sky that includes the circled objects.

Home Activity: Your child identified things that can be seen in a nighttime sky. With your child, draw a picture of a nighttime sky. Talk about what you can see in the nighttime sky that you cannot see in the daytime sky.

Lesson 4

What are some kinds of weather?

The weather can change every day.
The weather may be sunny, cloudy, windy, rainy, or snowy.
You can show the weather on a calendar.
Show what the weather is like today.

April

Sunday	Monday	Tuesday	Wednesday	Thursday	Friday	Saturday
				1	2	3
4	5	6	7	8	9	10
11	12	13	14	15	16	17
18	19	20	21	22	23	24
25	26	27	28	29	30	

myscienceonLine.com

THE BIG ? What are Earth and the sky like?

Lesson 4 Name ______________________

What are some kinds of weather?

Color the picture that best shows what the weather is like today.

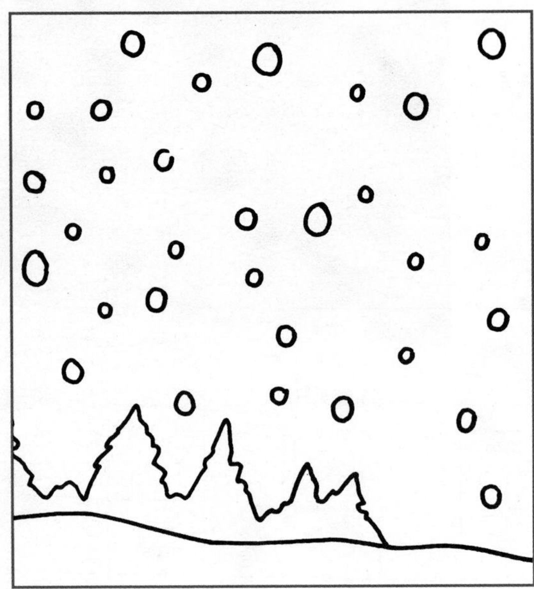

Directions: Look at the pictures with children. Discuss the type of weather each picture shows and the weather children observed today. Then have them color the picture that best matches today's weather.

Home Activity: Discuss these kinds of weather with your child: sunny, cloudy, windy, rainy, and snowy. Have your child draw a picture of himself or herself outdoors in today's weather.

Lesson 5

What are the seasons?

The seasons may have different kinds of weather.
Summer may be hot.
Fall may be cool.
Winter may be cold.
Spring may be warm.
Tell about the seasons where you live.

summer

mysciencеonline.com

THE BIG ? What are Earth and the sky like?

Lesson 5

Name ________________________________

What are the seasons?

Color the picture of winter blue.

Color the picture of summer yellow.

Color the picture of spring green.

Color the picture of fall red.

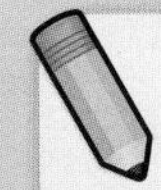

Directions: Discuss with children the seasons and different kinds of weather associated with each season. Have children color something in each seasonal picture with the color named for that season.

Home Activity: Discuss with your child how your region is affected by the seasons. Then help your child draw a picture showing a favorite season.

Investigate It!

What do the day and night skies look like?

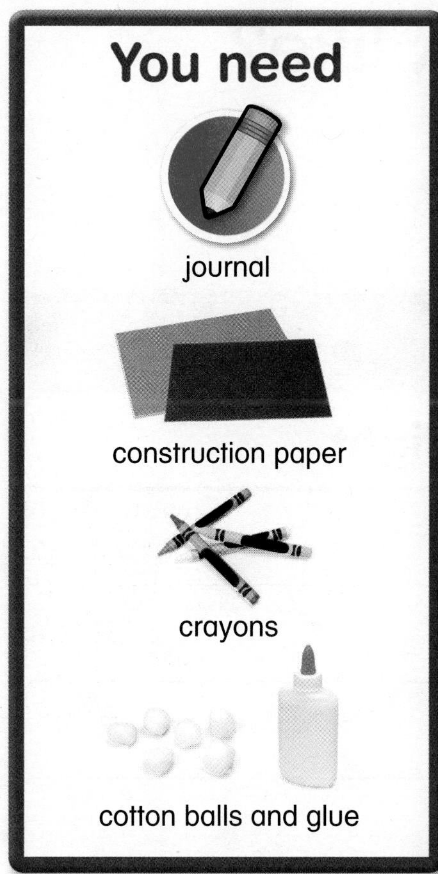

You need
journal
construction paper
crayons
cotton balls and glue

1 Label.

2 Make.

3 Compare.

4 Write.

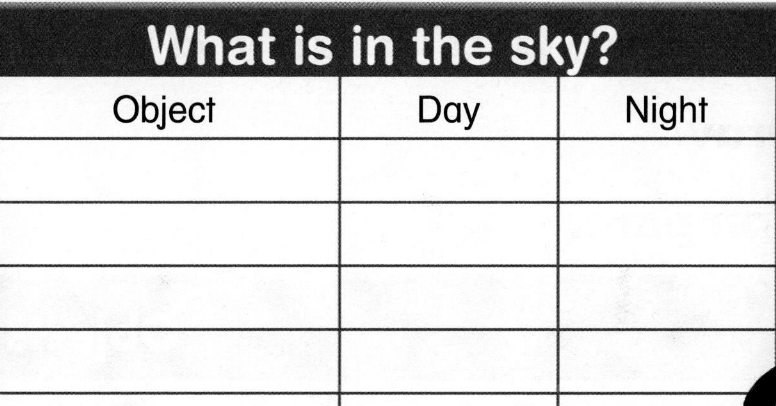

What is in the sky?		
Object	Day	Night

myscienceonline.com

Name ____________________

Inquiry **Investigate It!**

What do the day and night skies look like?

Draw.

Compare.

Objects in the Sky

Object	Day	Night

Directions: Have children draw their pictures in the "Object" column. Have them look at their pictures. Have them use check marks to show which objects are visible during the day, which are visible at night, and which are visible at both times.

Big World My World

Ready for the Weather

People learn about the weather across the country.

You learn about the weather too. What do you do to get ready for rainy weather?

Big World

My World

THE BIG ? What are Earth and the sky like?

myscienceonline.com

Name ____________________

Ready for the Weather

Color the picture that shows what you could wear and use on a hot summer day.

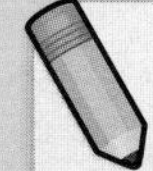

Directions: Identify the items in each small picture, and have children color the picture with items that are most appropriate for a hot summer day.

Home Activity: Watch or listen to a weather report with your child. Then choose clothes he or she might wear outdoors given the day's weather.

Ohio

Unit

D

Physical Science

Chapter 5
Objects

What are objects like?

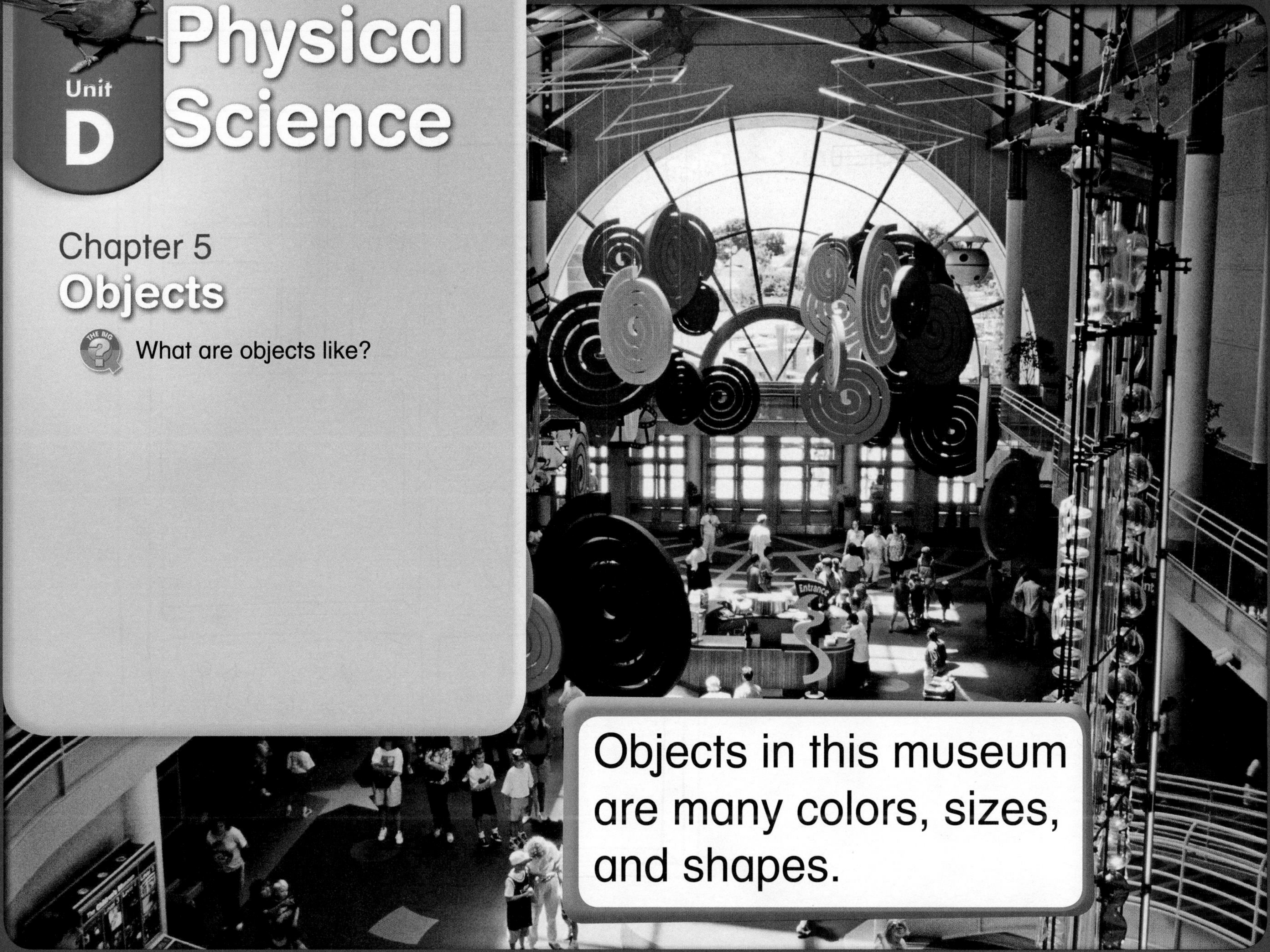

Objects in this museum are many colors, sizes, and shapes.

Ohio

Name ______________________________

Physical Science

Circle the dinosaur in the picture.

Color the picture.

Directions: Discuss the picture with children. Ask children to circle the dinosaur on the page. Then have them color the picture. Discuss how the dinosaur and the other things on the page are all objects.

Home Activity: Your child is going to study physical science. He or she will learn about objects. Select an object in your home, such as a toy. Ask your child to tell about the object's shape, color, and size. Repeat with other items.

Ohio

Chapter 5

Objects

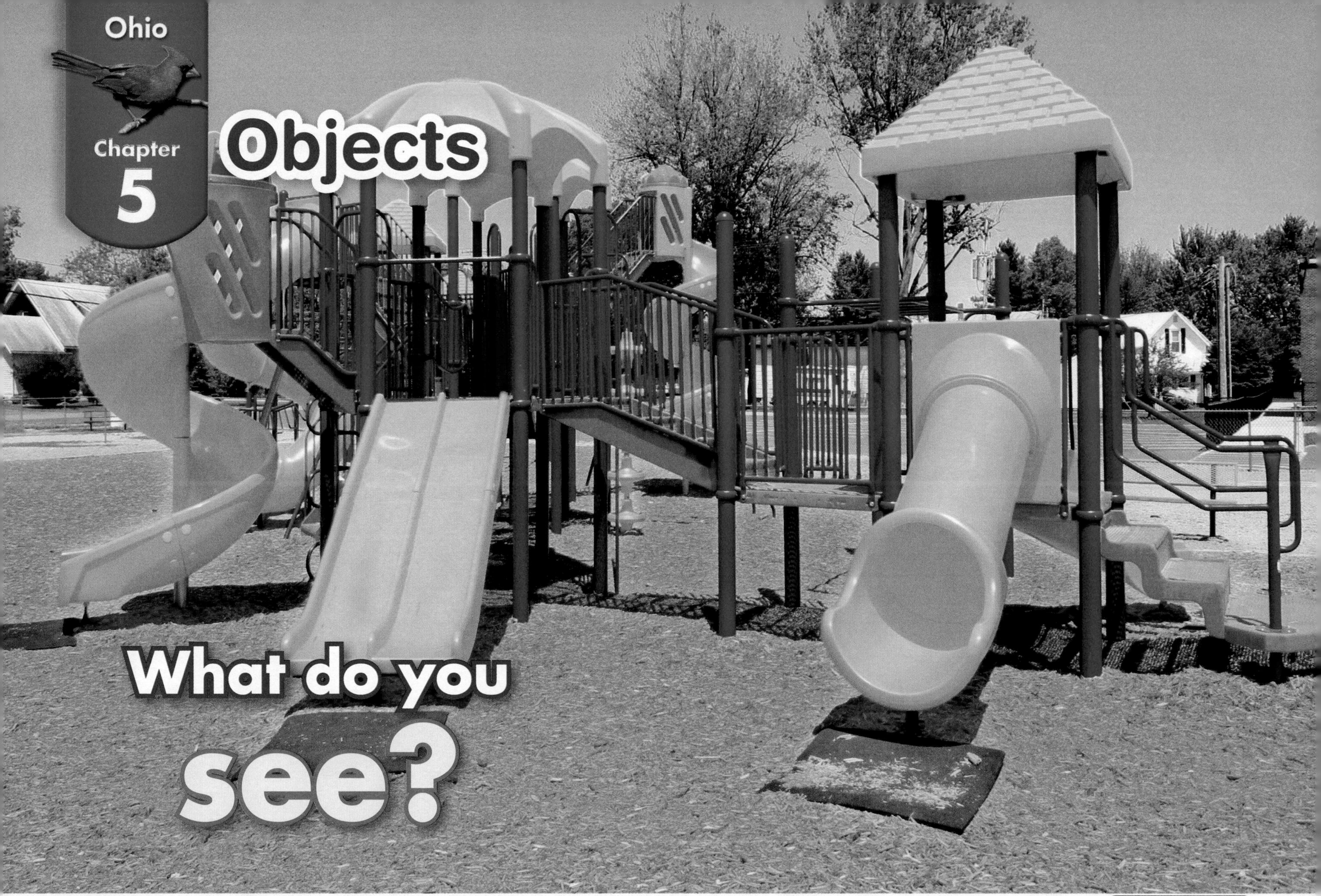

What do you see?

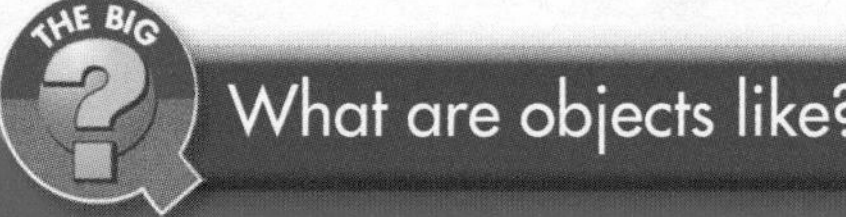

What are objects like?

Ohio

Name ____________________

What are objects like?

Look at the pictures below.

Circle the pictures of things you might find at a playground.

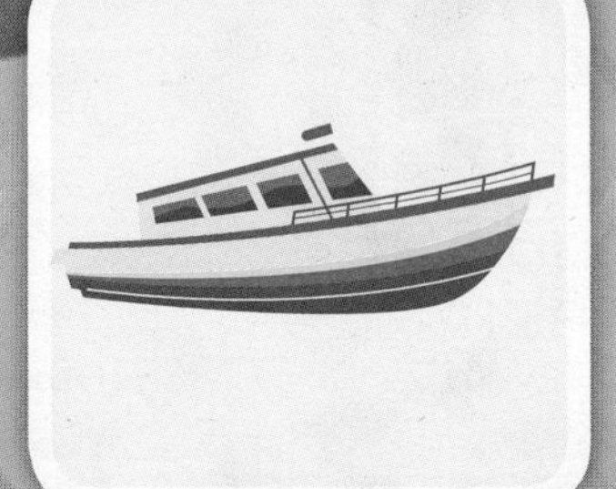

Draw a picture.

Show what you like to do at the playground.

Activity 44
Use with page 44.

Directions: Have children circle the pictures of things they might see at a playground. Then have children draw a picture of themselves on their favorite playground equipment.

Home Activity: In Chapter 6, your child will learn about matter and its properties. Point to an object in your home, and help your child describe it by asking questions such as, "Is it big or little?" "Is it red or blue?"

Inquiry **Try It!**

How can you sort objects?

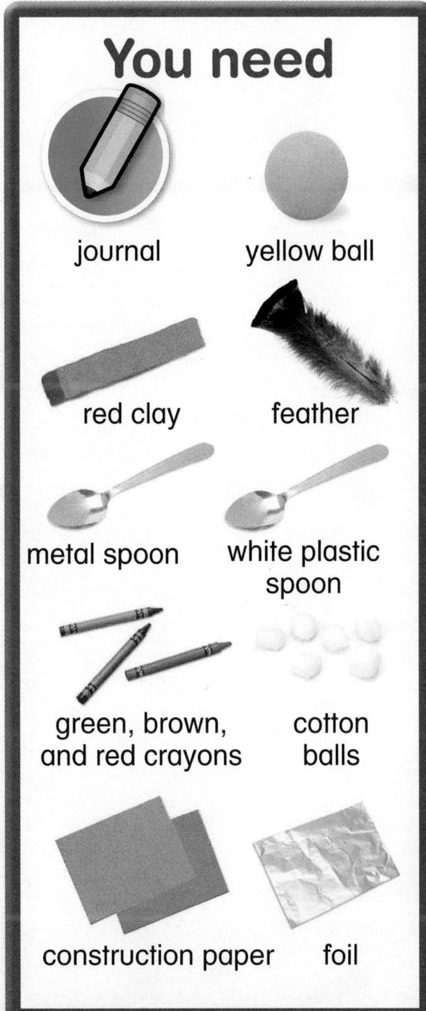

You need
journal
yellow ball
red clay
feather
metal spoon
white plastic spoon
green, brown, and red crayons
cotton balls
construction paper
foil

1 Look.

2 Touch.

3 Sort.

4 Write.

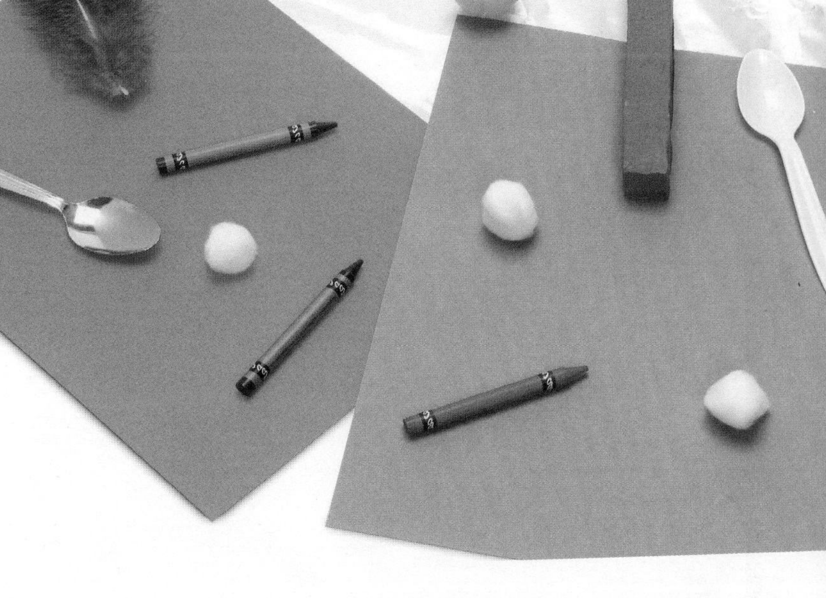

myscienceonline.com

Name ______________________________

Inquiry **Try It!**

How can you sort objects?

Draw.

Activity 45
Use with page 45.

Directions: Have children draw a set of objects that are alike.

Let's Read Science!

Main Idea and Details

This statue is a fountain.

The fountain sprays water.

The fountain has many colors.

Tell about the fountain.

mysciencEonline.com

THE BIG ? What are objects like?

Name ______________________________

Main Idea and Details

Color one boat green.

Color one boat red.

Color one boat brown.

Color the sun yellow.

Count the boats.

Write the number.

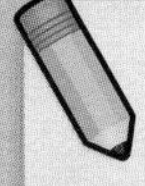

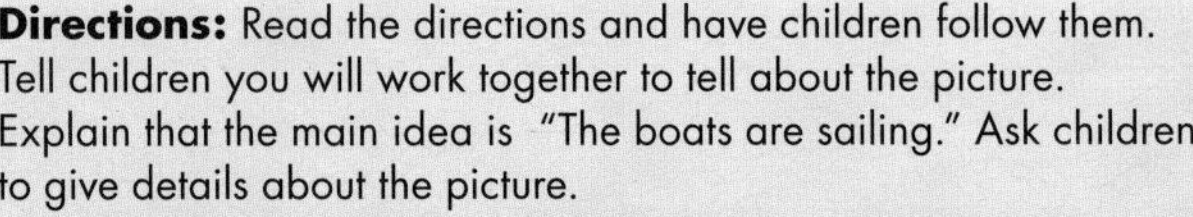

Directions: Read the directions and have children follow them. Tell children you will work together to tell about the picture. Explain that the main idea is "The boats are sailing." Ask children to give details about the picture.

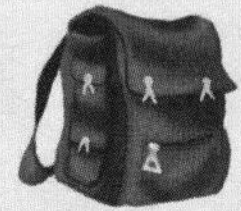

Tell your child how you use a room in your home. ("We use the kitchen to prepare and eat meals.") Ask your child to tell a detail about the room. Your child might say, "The kitchen has a stove." Encourage your child to give lots of details.

Lesson 1

What are your five senses?

You have five senses. You use your senses to learn.

see

hear

smell

taste

touch

myscienceonline.com

THE BIG ? What are objects like?

Lesson 1

Name ______________________________

What are your five senses?

Draw a line to match each sense word with the correct picture.

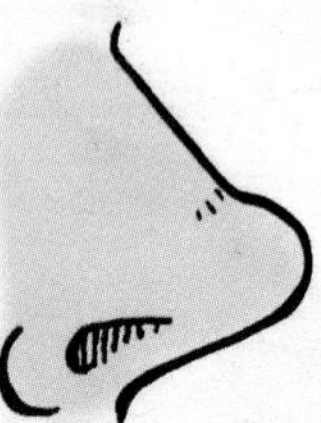
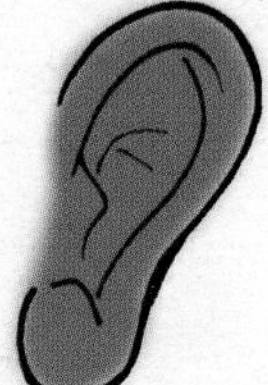

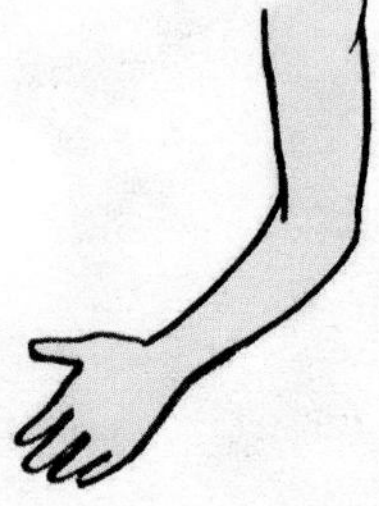
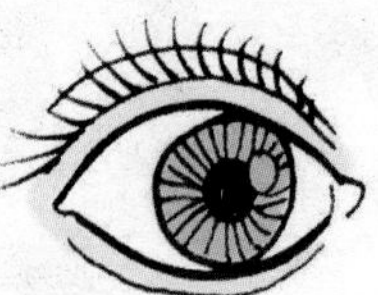

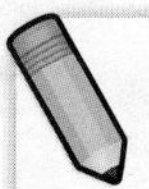

Directions: Read the sense words to children. Help them identify the pictures. Discuss which picture goes with each sense word. Have children draw lines to match the sense words with the appropriate pictures.

Home Activity: Point to your eyes and say, "I use my eyes to ____." Have your child complete the sentence with the appropriate sense word: "I use my eyes to see." Continue with your ears, nose, mouth/ tongue, and hands.

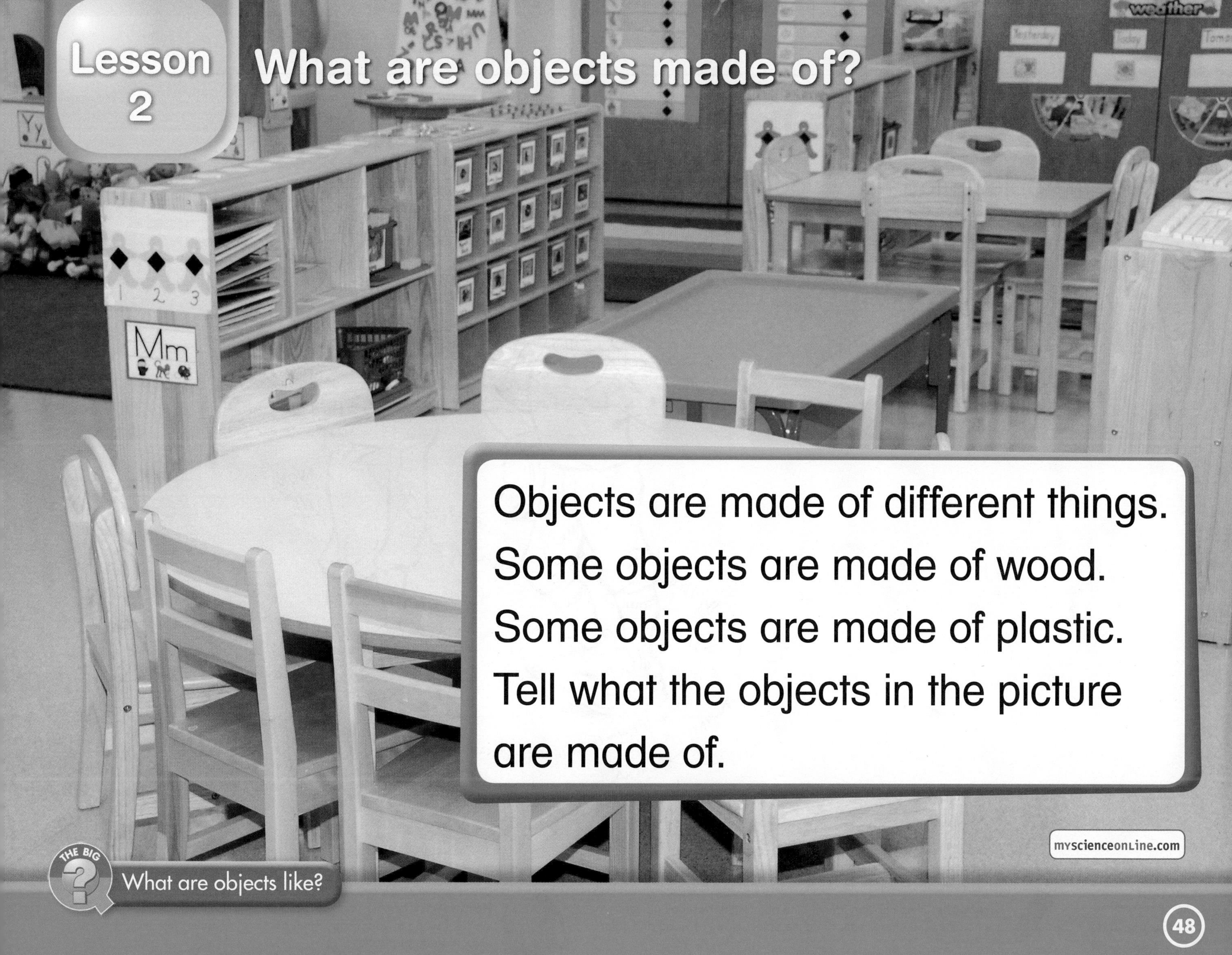

Lesson 2 What are objects made of?

Objects are made of different things.
Some objects are made of wood.
Some objects are made of plastic.
Tell what the objects in the picture are made of.

THE BIG ? What are objects like?

Lesson 2

Name ____________________

What are objects made of?

Circle the object made of wood.

Color the picture.

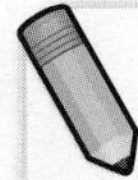

Directions: Help children identify the objects the baseball players are holding. Then have them circle the object made of wood and color the picture.

Home Activity: Ask your child to find and name two objects made of wood in your home. Then ask them to name two objects made of plastic.

Lesson 3 What can you tell about objects?

You can group objects.
Objects can be different sizes and shapes.
Objects can be many different colors.
Some objects are heavy.
Some objects are light.

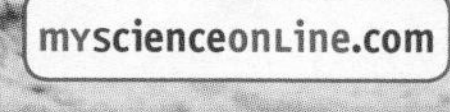

THE BIG ? What are objects like?

Lesson 3

Name ______________________

What can you tell about objects?

Circle the things that are heavy.

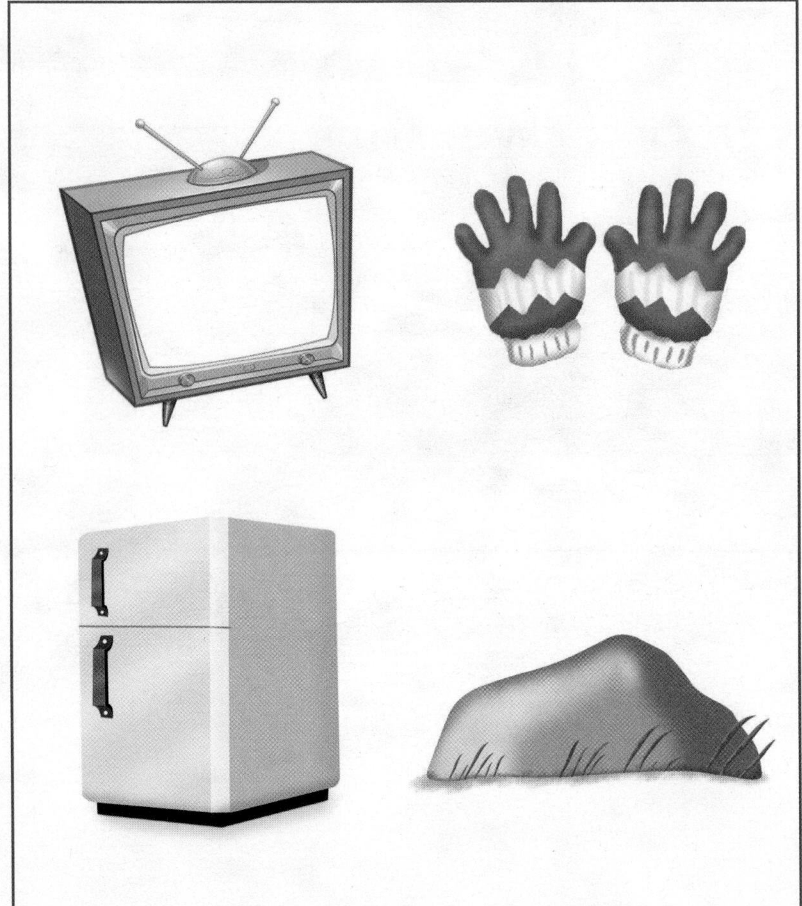

Circle the things that are light.

Activity 49
Use with page 49.

Directions: Help children name the objects in the top box. Have them circle the heavy objects. Repeat the process for the bottom box, but ask children to circle the light objects.

Home Activity: Give your child an object, such as a dinner plate. Ask your child to describe the object using as many words as possible. Then have him or her tell whether the object is heavy or light.

Lesson 4 How can you sort objects?

You can sort by size.
You can sort by weight.
You can sort by how objects feel.

THE BIG ? What are objects like?

Lesson 4 Name ______________________________

How can you sort objects?

Color the biggest object in each picture.

Directions: Remind children that one way to sort objects is by size. Help them identify the stacking dolls in the first picture and tell them to color the biggest one. Repeat the process for the other pictures.

Home Activity: Have fun sorting objects with your child. You might sort objects, such as books, by size. You might sort objects, such as balls, by weight. You might sort objects that are soft or hard.

How is sound made?

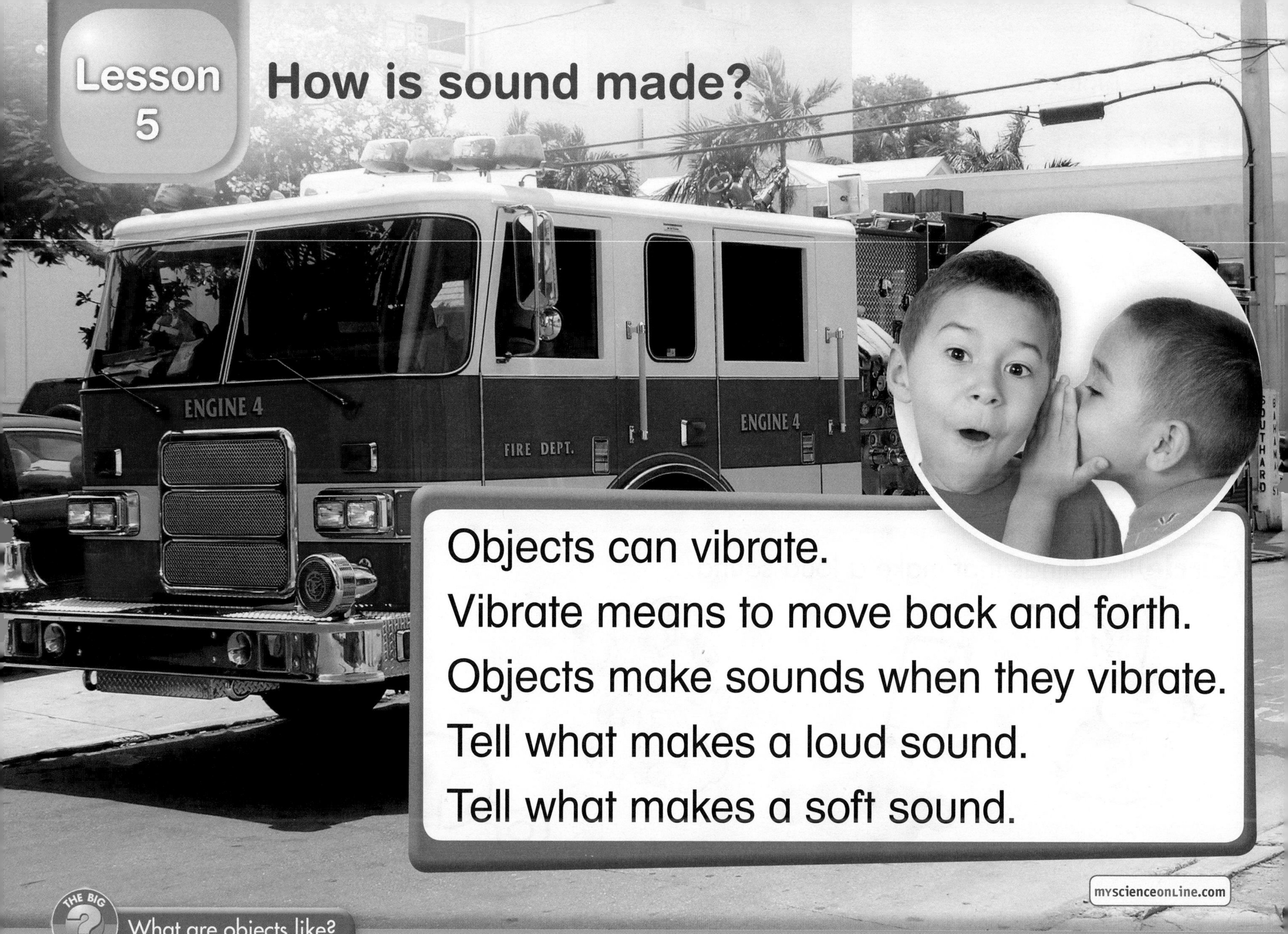

Objects can vibrate.

Vibrate means to move back and forth.

Objects make sounds when they vibrate.

Tell what makes a loud sound.

Tell what makes a soft sound.

myscienceonLine.com

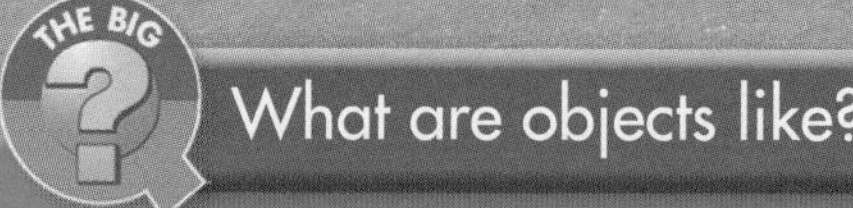
THE BIG ?
What are objects like?

Lesson 5

Name ______________________________

How is sound made?

Circle the things that make a soft sound.

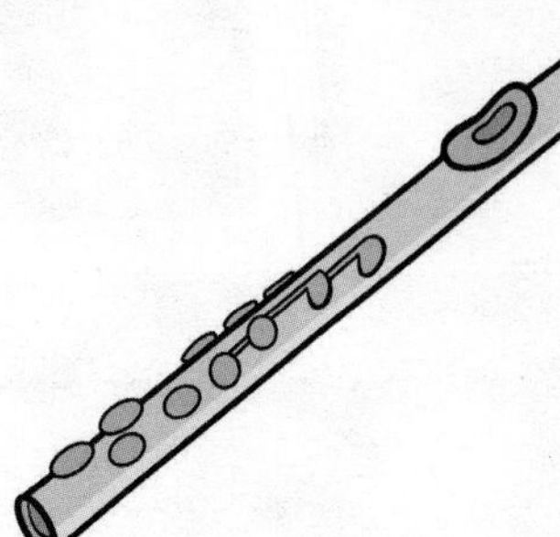

Circle the things that make a loud sound.

Directions: Have children identify the pictures in the first box. Ask which pictures show things that make soft sounds. Have children circle those things. Proceed in the same way with the second set of pictures, asking children to identify and circle things that make loud sounds.

Home Activity: Have your child identify loud and soft sounds that you might hear at home. For example, a ticking clock makes a soft sound, but a truck rumbling down the street might make a loud sound.

Inquiry Investigate It!

Which object is heavier?

You need
journal
balance with cups
hand lens and clay
rubber ball and table-tennis ball

1 Put.

2 Look.

3 Write.

4 Put.

5 Look.

myscienceonline.com

Name ____________________

Inquiry **Investigate It!**

Which object is heavier?

Look. Which is heavier?

Draw.

Crayon or Spoon	Hand Lens or Clay	Rubber Ball or Table Tennis Ball

Directions: Have children place the items in the cups on the balance, then draw the item that is heavier.

Count
Count the red toys.
Count the toys with wheels.
Count the toys that are soft.
Do the math!
SCHOOL BUS
myscienceonline.com
THE BIG ?
What are objects like?

Name ____________________

Count

Write a number to answer each question.

How many soft toys are there?

____

How many round toys are there?

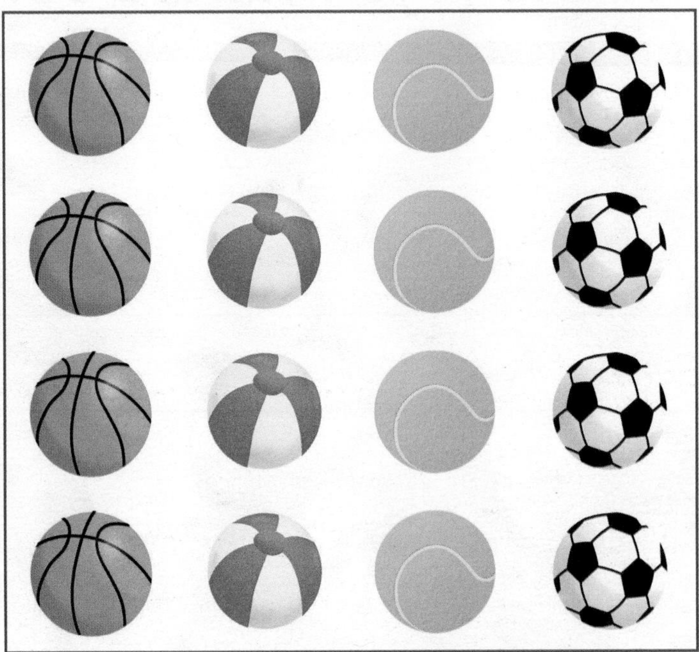

____

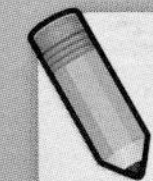
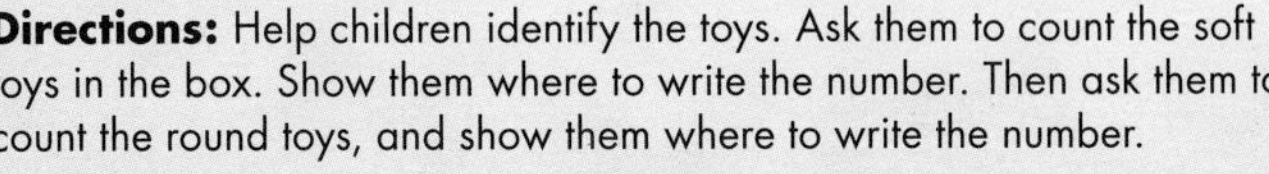

Directions: Help children identify the toys. Ask them to count the soft toys in the box. Show them where to write the number. Then ask them to count the round toys, and show them where to write the number.

Home Activity: Your child has learned how to count groups of objects that are alike. Line up items, such as pennies, on a table. Have your child count the items.

Credits

Staff Credits

The people who made up the ***Interactive Science*** team—representing composition services, core design digital and multimedia production services, digital product development, editorial, editorial services, manufacturing, and production—are listed below.

Geri Amani, Alisa Anderson, Jose Arrendondo, Amy Austin, David Bailis, Scott Baker, Lindsay Bellino, Charlie Bink, Bridget Binstock, Holly Blessen, Robin Bobo, Craig Bottomley, Jim Brady, Laura Brancky, Chris Budzisz, Odette Calderon, Sitha Chhor, Mary Chingwa, Caroline Chung, Margaret Clampitt, Kier Cline, Brandon Cole, Mitch Coulter, AnnMarie Coyne, Fran Curran, Dana Damiano, Michael Di Maria, Nancy Duffner, Amanda Ferguson, David Gall, Mark Geyer, Amy Goodwin, Gerardine Griffin, Chris Haggerty, Margaret Hall, Laura Hancko, Christian Henry, Autumn Hickenlooper, Guy Huff, George Jacobson, Marian Jones, Kathi Kalina, Chris Kammer, Sheila Kanitsch, Alyse Kondrat, Mary Kramer, Thea Limpus, Dominique Mariano, Lori McGuire, Melinda Medina, Angelina Mendez, Claudi Mimo, John Moore, Kevin Mork, Chris Niemyjski, Phoebe Novak, Anthony Nuccio, Jeff Osier, Charlene Rimsa, Rebecca Roberts, Camille Salerno, Manuel Sanchez, Carol Schmitz, Amanda Seldera, Sheetal Shah, Jeannine Shelton El, Geri Shulman, Greg Sorenson, Samantha Sparkman, Mindy Spelius, Karen Stockwell, Dee Sunday, Dennis Tarwood, Jennie Teece, Lois Teesdale, Michaela Tudela, Karen Vuchichevich, Barbara Watters, Tom Wickland, James Yagelski, Tim Yetzina, Diane Zimmermann

Illustrations

ACT1, ACT49 Ron Berg; **ACT4, ACT13, ACT51** Bob Ostrom; **ACT4, ACT5, ACT6, ACT9, ACT20, ACT23, ACT24, ACT28, ACT31, ACT36, ACT57, ACT65, ACT84** Jenny B Harris; **ACT4, ACT9, ACT12, ACT18, ACT20, ACT49** Ken Gamage; **ACT4, ACT12, ACT20, ACT51** Remy Simard; **ACT5, ACT12, ACT13, ACT36, ACT38** John Haslam; **ACT5, ACT28** Paul Sharp; **ACT5, ACT12, ACT24, ACT28, ACT53** Robin Boyer; **ACT6, ACT18, ACT36, ACT51** Chris Lensch; **ACT6, ACT37** Julia Woolf; **ACT9, ACT44** Jim Steck; **ACT9, ACT12, ACT13, ACT18** Leslie Harrington; **ACT9, ACT12** Michael Moran; **ACT12, ACT23** Holli Conger; **ACT24, ACT53** Luciana Navarro Powell; **ACT24** Sheree Boyd; **ACT36, ACT38** Sam Ward; Scott Burroughs; **ACT51** Jackie Stafford; **ACT44** Brenda Sexton; **ACT48** Dean MacAdam; **ACT48** Geoffrey Paul Smith.

Photographs

Every effort has been made to secure permission and provide appropriate credit for photographic material. The publisher deeply regrets any omission and pledges to correct errors called to its attention in subsequent editions.

Unless otherwise acknowledged, all photographs are the property of Pearson Education, Inc.

Photo locators denoted as follows: Top (T), Center (C), Bottom (B), Left (L), Right (R), Background (Bkgd)

Cover

1 (Bkgrd) ©James Thew/Shutterstock, (Bkgrd) ©niderlander/Shutterstock, Jose Luis Pelaez/Getty Images; **2** Photolibrary Group, Inc.; **4** (T) ©Masterfile Royalty-Free; **5** ©Ian Scott/Shutterstock; **6** (BL) ©GAmut Stock Images Pvt Ltd Gamut/Alamy, (TR) ©PhotoAlto/Alamy, (BR) ©Westend61 GmbH/Alamy, (TL) Getty Images; **9** (TR) Jupiter Images; **10** (Bkgrd) ©Shannon Fagan/Getty Images; **12** Christen Wooley; **15** DKCenteraTest/©DK Images; **16** (R) ©Fancy Collection/SuperStock; **17** (Bkgrd) ©Asia Images Group/Getty Images, (BL) ©Dean Sanderson/Getty Images; **18** (R, L, C) ©Anton Vengo/SuperStock; **20** ©Blend Images/SuperStock, (Inset) ©Frank Miller/Time & Life Pictures/Getty Images; **22** ©Frank Cezus/Getty Images; **23** ©Big Cheese Photo/Jupiter Images; **25** (BL) ©Chris Hepburn/Getty Images, (Bkgrd) ©image100/Jupiter Images, (TL) ©Kenneth Jones/Alamy, (BR) ©Shem Compion/Getty Images, (TCR) ©WaterFrame/Alamy; **26** ©Pierre Rosberg/Getty Images; **27** (Inset) ©ImageState/Alamy Images, ©Keren Su/Getty Images; **28** (BCL) ©American Images Inc/Getty Images, (TCR) ©Frans Lemmens/Corbis, (BL) ©Leighton Photography & Imaging/Shutterstock, (TR) ©Rolf Nussbaumer/Nature Picture Library, (BR) Jupiter Images; **29** (BC) ©Casey K. Bishop/Shutterstock, (TR) ©Charlene Bayerle/Shutterstock, (Bkgrd) Photolibrary Group, Inc., (BL) Photos to Go/Photolibrary; **30** (BL) ©John Martin Will/Shutterstock, (TCL) ©Lisa a. Svara/Shutterstock, (TR) ©Steve Byland/Shutterstock; **31** ©Jeff Greenberg/Alamy Images; **32** © Alexey Stiop/Shutterstock; **33** ©Jozsef Szasz-Fabian/Shutterstock; **35** ©Joe Fox/Alamy; **36** (TC) ©Datacraft/Getty Images, (Bkgrd) ©Doug Chinnery/Getty Images, (BR) ©Steve Allen/Getty Images; **37** ©Galyna Andrushko/Shutterstock; **38** Photolibrary Group, Inc.; **39** ©Digitaler Lumpensammier/Getty Images; **40** (TR) ©Glen Allison/Getty Images, (TC) ©Purestock/Getty Images, (BC) ©Steve Satushek/Getty Images; **42** (Bkgrd) ©Dennis MacDonald/Alamy/Alamy Images, (Inset) Jupiter Images; **43** ©Jack Schiffer/Shutterstock; **45** ©claudio h. artman/Alamy; **49** ©redcover/Getty Images; **50** (Bkgrd) ©Mario Savoia/Shutterstock, (BCR) ©Tiplyashin Anatoly/Shutterstock, (Inset) Shutterstock;

Ohio Learn More About It!

Page OH6

Page OH5

Page OH8
Page OH3
Page OH2
Page OH2

Name ______________________________

Where Plants and Animals Live

Different plants and animals live in different places.

Gila monsters are a kind of animal.

Cactuses are a kind of plant.

Gila monsters and cactuses live in a desert.

Sea grass is a kind of plant.

Dugongs are a kind of animal.

Dugongs and sea grass live in the ocean.

Tell how Gila monsters and dugongs are alike and different.

Tell how cactuses and sea grass are alike and different.

Living things are found almost everywhere in the world. There are somewhat different kinds in different places.

Name ______________________________ **Learn More About It!**

What Helps Living Things

The way plants and animals act helps them live.

The parts of plants and animals help them live too.

Dogs need food to live.

Dogs have teeth for chewing food.

Trees need food to live.

Leaves make food for the tree.

A trunk holds the leaves up.

Draw an X on what holds the leaves up.

Circle what the dog uses to chew food.

Tell how the other parts of the dog help it live.

Living things are made up of a variety of structures. Some of these structures and behaviors influence their survival.

Name ____________________ **Learn More About It!**

Air and Wind

Air is all around Earth.

Air is nonliving.

You might feel wind blow outside.

Wind is moving air.

Wind moves the pinwheels in the picture.

Tell about air.

Circle what the wind moves.

 Air is a nonliving substance that surrounds Earth, wind is moving air.

Name ______________________________ Learn More About It!

Weather Changes

Temperature is how hot or cold something is.

You can measure temperature with a thermometer.

The temperature outside tells about the weather.

The temperature can change every day.

The temperature might be cold today.

The temperature might be warmer tomorrow.

Tell how the temperature changed from Tuesday to Wednesday.

Tell how you know.

Wind, temperature and precipitation document short-term weather changes.

Name ______________________ Learn More About It!

Stars

You can see stars in the sky at night.

Sometimes you can see stars in the sky in the early morning.

Evening is between day and night.

Sometimes you can see stars in the sky in the evening.

Some stars look brighter than other stars.

Circle the two brightest stars.

Write if the picture shows day or night.

____

Stars are visible at night, some are visible in the evening or morning, and some are brighter than others.

Name ____________________

The Shape of the Moon

You can see the moon in the night sky.

The shape of the moon looks different each night.

The shape of the moon looks like it slowly changes.

It seems to change every night during the month.

Next month the moon will look like it does tonight.

Tell how the shape of the moon looks from night to night.

Draw what the moon will look like one month from now.

The observable shape of the moon changes in size very slowly throughout each day of every month.

Name ________________________________ Learn More About It!

The Sun and the Seasons

The sun is in a different position in the sky each season.

The sun is low in the sky in winter.

The sun is higher in the sky in spring and fall.

The sun is highest in the sky in summer.

Circle when the sun is highest.

Put an X on when the sun is lowest.

winter

spring

summer

fall

The sun's position in the sky change in a single day and from season to season.

Name ____________________ Learn More About It!

Making Sound

You can make sound in many ways.

You can blow across the top of a bottle to make sound.

You can tap a drum to make sound.

Different drums make different sounds.

A small drum makes a higher sound than a big drum.

Tell how these children make sound.

Tell how you can touch something to make sound.

Sound is produced by touching, blowing or tapping objects. The sounds that are produced vary depending on the properties of objects.

Credits

Photographs

Every effort has been made to secure permission and provide appropriate credit for photographic material. The publisher deeply regrets any omission and pledges to correct errors called to its attention in subsequent editions.

Unless otherwise acknowledged, all photographs are the property of Pearson Education, Inc.

Photo locators denoted as follows: Top (T), Center (C), Bottom (B), Left (L), Right (R), Background (Bkgd)

OH0 (Bkgrd) ©marilyn barbone/Shutterstock, (CL) ©violetkaipa/Shutterstock, (BL) Jupiterimages/Thinkstock; OH1 (TCR) ©ableimages/Alamy Images, (BCR) ©Joe Belanger/Shutterstock, (BR) ©Martin Strmiska/Alamy, (TR) ©R. Gino Santa Maria/Shutterstock; OH2 (TR) ©Joe Belanger/Shutterstock, (CR) ©Martin Strmiska/Alamy, (Bkgrd) ©Rich Carey/Shutterstock, (TCL) Jupitrimages/Thinkstock; OH3 (TR) ©ableimages/Alamy Images, ©marilyn barbone/Shutterstock; OH4 (Bkgrd) Juice Images/Glow Images; OH5 (TR) ©Tracy Whiteside/Shutterstock, (BR) Jupiterimages/Thinkstock; OH6 ©violetkaipa/Shutterstock; OH7 (B) John Sanford/Photo Researchers, Inc.; OH8 (BR) ©Elenamiv/Shutterstock, (BCL) ©Fedorov Oleksly/Shutterstock, (BCR) ©R. Gino Santa Maria/Shutterstock, (BL) Shutterstock; OH9 ©Image Source ; OH10 (CL) ©Image Source , (Bkgrd) Juice Images/Glow Images, (TC) Jupitrimages/Thinkstock.

About Science

Draw pictures. Write words.

About Science

About Science

About Science

About Science

About Science

About Science